CELEBRATING WRITERS AND WRITING IN OUR COMMUNITIES

An Anthology of the Winning Entries of the Redwood Writers Contest of 2025

Redwood Council of Teachers of English

Redwood Writing Project

Celebrating Writers and Writing in our Communities: An Anthology of the Winning Entries of the Redwood Writers Contest of 2025

© 2025 Redwood Council of Teachers of English

Cover original artwork by Lauren House.

Published by:
The Press at Cal Poly Humboldt
Cal Poly Humboldt Library
1 Harpst Street
Arcata, CA 95521-8299
digitalcommons.humboldt.edu

ISBN: 978-1-962081-29-0
ISSN: 2767-2700

About this Anthology

Celebrating Writers and Writing in Our Communities is an anthology that includes the award winning works of students grades 3rd through 12th in Humboldt County and the surrounding area. The journal is available in digital format at digitalcommons.humboldt.edu and as a printed, bound copy through Amazon.com.

The annual writing contest is co-sponsored by the Redwood Council of Teachers of English, an affiliate of the California Association of Teachers of English, and the Redwood Writing Project. Student entries are submitted to the Redwood Writing Contest at the Redwood Writing Project website (rwp.humboldt.edu) in order to be considered.

This anthology is published annually at the conclusion of the annual Redwood CATE Writing Contest to showcase its award winning entries. Any student in the local area can submit to the appropriate category.

**This anthology is a publication sponsored by Redwood CATE
with combined support from Redwood Writing Project and
Cal Poly Humboldt Library.**

Acknowledgments

The Redwood Council of Teachers of English and the Redwood Writing Project thank the following individuals and organizations for their support of this writing contest:

- Humboldt Sponsors

- Kyle Morgan, Sarah Godlin, and student assistants, Cal Poly Humboldt Library

- Sarah Ben-Zvi, RWP employee and contest coordinator

- Lauren House, anthology artist and Cal Poly Humboldt student

Table of Contents

Poetry   Page

Grades 3 & 4

1st place--I Start to Dance by Morning Star Dean 2
1st place--Sports by Dean Rasmussen 3
2nd place (tie)--How I Feel About Pop Culture by Emmett Brown 4
2nd place (tie)--Ballet by Ella Koch 5
3rd place--I Live in a Place Called Hoopa by K'Oden White 6
Honorable Mention--Pala California by Kautia Hostler 7
Honorable Mention--I Am From Hoopa by Oscar Colegrove 8

Grades 5 & 6

1st place--The Hupa Boxer by Xavien Ruiz 9
2nd place--Acorns and Beargrass by Vivian Hailey 11

Grades 7 & 8

1st place--Right Time, Right Girl by Zuma Kan 12
2nd place--Known by Camille Tyner 14

Grades 9 & 10

1st place (tie)--The Man Behind the Music by Anaia Benneman 15
1st place (tie)--Not Fully There by Kona Bettenhausen 17
2nd place (tie)--Society's Fleeting Glow by Meilin Storm 19
2nd place (tie)--Privileged by Kloe Bryant 20
3rd place--Social Media Arch by Bella DeCarli 21

Grades 11 & 12

1st place (tie)--Distractions by Juniper Otter 22
1st place (tie)--Human by Greg Pronovost-Carlson 25
1st place (tie)--The Generation of Magpies by Fiona Smart 30
2nd place (tie)--High School Graduation by Dulce Ramos 32
2nd place (tie)--Echoes of the Night Before by Autumn Hudgens 35
3rd place (tie)--The Purpose of Music by Peyton Ellis Studebaker 38
3rd place (tie)--Thin to Win by Lilian Mion 40

Short Story   Page

Grades 5 & 6

1st place--The Last Pearl by Elizabeth Gibbons 42
2nd place--Andrew's Rise of Soccer by Whilhelmina Luna 47
3rd place--We Don't Care by June Wickman 48

Grades 9 & 10

1st place(tie)--Reflections by Symon Mendoza 49
1st place (tie)--Blue Light by Eliza Lehman 54
1st place (tie)--Lacy's Blue Summer by Josephine Maguire 58
2nd place (tie)--I Am Batman by Dylan Frecks 66
2nd place (tie)--Impractical Lives by Paula Licea Ortiz 68
2nd place (tie)--Music is Soul: A Sublime Tale by Eva Cox 70
3rd place--A Funny Guy, A Dark Topic, A look, and the Boy by Sawyer Robert Pixley 72

Short Essay   Page

Grades 3 & 4

1st place--How Lego Has Affected My Life by Richard Schnur 76
2nd place--Amazing Bunnies by Wenyu Cao 77
3rd place--Culture and Art by May Belle O'Connell 78

Grades 5 & 6

1st place--Left Out From Your World by Cicada Pierce 79
2nd place--Greta Thunberg by Penn Kerhoulas 81

Grades 7 & 8

1st place (tie)--Female Athlete Trailblazers by Maple Myers 82
1st place (tie)--How Anime Changed My Life by Carissa Gonzalez 84
2nd place (tie)--Trophy Crazy by Bodhi Koger 86
2nd place (tie)--Empire of Knowledge by Zuma Kan 88
3rd place (tie)--Play for the Experience and Not the Outcome by William Simms Jr. 90
3rd place (tie)--The Impact by BellaAnn King 92

Grades 9 & 10

1st place (tie)--Snapchat: The Social Scandal by Skylar Groff 93
1st place (tie)--Political Media and How it Had an Effect on Me by Rilynn Sauber 95
2nd place--Mental Disorders in Media and My Experience by Sarah Barsanti 97
3rd place--The Instagram Effect by Jaxon Davis 100
Honorable Mention--Did You Know by Cameron Hayden-Davi 104

Grades 11 & 12

1st place (tie)--How Pop Culture Shaped Me by Humphrey Mbugua 106
1st place (tie)--Black is Beautiful by Fallyn Miller 109
1st place (tie)--Women in Pop Culture by Evelynn Snow 111
2nd place (tie)--The Impact VSCO Girls Had on Society by Shyla Mosier 114
2nd place (tie)--Pop Culture: A Short Essay by Patti Henderson 116
2nd place (tie)--Anti-Social Media by Cole Zeller 119
3rd place (tie)--Social Motivation by Alex Jimenez 122
3rd place (tie)--The Influence of Sports Betting by Dallin Baker 124

Poetry

I Start to Dance

by Morning Star Dean

I start to dance

when Sabrina Carpenter

plays on the radio I start to dance

when my favorite song comes on

I start to dance

me and my sister dance when

her favorite song comes on

when her song comes on I start to dance

when I hear music I start to dance

I hear music and it makes me feel like I am alive

sometimes I like to dance with a rose and sometimes I like to dance

with my sister and when I dance

with my sister it's because I don't want to dance

alone

Sports

by Dean Rasmussen

Basketball,Soccer,Baseball and Football
Brings me Strength and Confidence
Brings me Happiness and Love
Do you see me playing Sports?

Sports taught me to keep Pushing
It taught me to always Remember that
You are Great, You can do this, You got
this You got this, thinking of Myself
Playing professionally
I Believe in my Friends, my Family and especially Me

Sports isn't just about the gear It's about having Fun
Some people have thousands of dollars of gear
Some a couple dollars
I would be happy with either
Some of my friends are really good in mostly every Sport
I teach them and all the Sports they learned by themselves

All of my friends know many Sports
Even if they hadn't heard of them
My family has some of the Best Sports Players I have Ever met

How I Feel About Pop Culture

by Emmett Brown

Fortnite can make me less stressed
Ranked, reload
Playing with your friends
Talk to your friends through a Microphone
Talk with each other and play at the same time

Movies can sometimes make me mad or sad
Characters sometimes do something stupid
Watching from the outside looking in

Brawl Stars, I love playing Brawl Stars with my dad
He is almost on the top of the leaderboard in the state

Sleep overs are so fun
Hang out with your family or friends
Play together
Sleepless nights

Ballet

by Ella Koch

Ballet makes me feel calm and relaxed
To me Ballet makes me feel like I'm flying
Like a beautiful morning bird
And I feel like I can fly with all the birds
Then I'm back to normal

But something just isn't right
Kind of in a good way
Kind of in a bad way
And I don't know what to do

And then I am alone
I like to listen to music during Ballet class
But to me the place I like to do Ballet is home
And now everything is all perfect
After that I do it again

I Live in a Place Called Hoopa

by K'Oden White

I live in a place called Hoopa
where people dance
and eat Native food like fish
and other Native stuff like eels
and find roots and sticks for baskets—
and another thing—
we dance
we dance in a deep pit and we sing
we wear feathers on our heads

I live in a place called Hoopa
where I watch TikTok in my bed
and roll myself up in my blanket
like a burrito
and eat potato chips
and hang out with my friends
drawing anime characters

always watching TikTok

Pala California

by Kautia Hostler

I like to watch people

sing

dance

and play sticks.

We went to Pala

My sister and I sang in the girls round for the first time

We sang in front of 300 people

 I was nervous

I got a sweater saying Native Love

and the girl that gave me the sweater

said when we sang

she cried

I Am From Hoopa

by Oscar Colegrove

Find some acorns
CRUSH them until there is only DUST left
Feed then to your Grandmas and Grandpas
      even to your sisters
I am from Hoopa
Put on your Hoopa regalia and start dancing
Learn the language from your sister
grow our population of speakers
I am from Hoopa

and watch the sun rise with me

I am from Hoopa
I like the Internet
There is so much to explore
Roblox, Fortnite,
Brawl, Stars and more!

The Hupa Boxer

by Xavien Ruiz

The bright lights, the crowd cheering, **BANG!** one hit **BANG!**
two hits **BANG!** three hits he's down…
One, two, he gets back up and then–

an alarm goes off–

He wakes up in a tent at the Brush Dance.

Come Get Your Feathers!

He hustles to the men's camp, gets suited up and heads into the pit,
the fire burning bright, the feathers swaying up and down, the smell of the root fills his
nose, takes him to another place, a calm place, a peaceful place.

He's jumping into the pit, the feathers swinging up, the hide in his left hand and his
jump stick in the right, the stars in the sky, the smoke rising, the dancers stomping,
the regalia shaking and rattling.

He's leaving for San Francisco. A boxing tournament. He sees his opponent. He's
intimidated. The two men step into the ring. The lights point to the ring. The big
screen shows the boxers.

Ding! Ding! Ding!

The match starts and he's praying

Dear Lord give me the strength to win this fight

Opening his eyes he approaches his opponent

BANG! one hit
BANG! two hits
BANG! three hits

A KNOCKOUT

Back home in Hoopa his family cheered.

He died forty years later.

Acorns and Bluegrass

by Vivian Hailey

I pick acorns and bear grass

With my aunty every year

and it is warm and cold

as I pick up the wet acorns.

My hands get dirtier and dirtier

Walking on the trail I see a creek

surrounded by bear grass

When we go home

I sit on the couch and

watch TikTok.

Right Time, Right Girl

by Zuma Kan

The great "American game"
The Game of Life?
Kendrick Lamar, do you want to play with us?

Why are we playing a game in a maze of contradictions?
In a world where we are "culturally divided,"
Choose multiplayer.
Why are we divided?
Why *aren't* we choosing multiplayer?
Does the game we are all "playing"
Have the ability to play multiplayer?
I <u>will</u> be in the room where it is being programmed.
I <u>will</u> take the computer and add multiplayer.
I <u>will</u> change the game.
How else will we win?

Described as, "too loud, too reckless, too ghetto."
Who's loud?
Who's reckless?
Who is ghetto?
Me?
Who gets to decide?
If *we* decide
Is it one experience that determines
If we are:
Loud,
Reckless,
Or ghetto?

How do we know if we are ready to play the game?
Do *we* get to decide as individuals?

Or do *we* get to decide as a society?
Why wouldn't *I* be ready?
Why *is* Lamar ready?
How can I be ready?
Changing my
Actions,
Thoughts,
Mindset?
Kendrick Lamar,
How do I play the game?

Known

by Camille Tyner

All she's ever known was lies disguised as love
But lies are where she's from
She can try to fake it
But she crumbles when she tries to commit
To one person
She can't even love without feeling like a burden
All She's ever known was manipulation
She feels hopeless in most situations
Strong in the others
But they even take that from her
She's known to be the perfect girl
But alone she rips at her curls
Trying to be strong
But ends up wanting to leave it all
So she seeks more love only to find out it's more lies
Can't find control so she just cries
Letting the tears flow
But once she's not alone
She finds the strength to smile and put on a show
It's all she's ever known

The Man Behind the Music

by Anaia Benemann

I've lived more lives
Than I can recall.
The song I love
Reminds me
Of a life
I have never lived.
Each day
I am living
In another's memory.

A familiar,
Melancholy,
Melody.
A "Dear Friend" from Somewhere out of reach. Sings of peace
And *love*.
Like a "'Blackbird' singing In the *dead of night.*"

I know not
The voice of the song I consume.
Yet I feel as though
The music knows me Better than I
Know myself.

The man behind the music Is so far away.
And yet,
His song is
At my fingertips
Each day.

I listen to the song I love In silence.
Between classes,
And through cold,
Dark,
Empty hallways

Not Fully There

by Kona Bettenhausen

Playing with marbles on the classroom carpet
They loved discussing their favorite things
Star Wars, Avengers, Transformers, Minecraft
"How do you not know?" they would ask

At the picnic table, they traded Pokémon cards
I could only stare off across the field
They lived in a different world than me
A world of celebrities and franchises
A world of imagination that I never understood
And in their gleeful company, I felt alone

This story didn't disappear as I matured
It only changed in representation
Social media is more important to my peers now
It invades conversations about the real world
Sentences are filled with allusions to TikTok trends
"Oh, I forgot you don't have social media," they say

And maybe it's bringing you down
Perhaps you spend hours on your phone
Wishing you could simply put it down
But for me, it's something I've never had
It's an escape from the real world
In my life, it has always been forbidden

So would you please tell me everything
Whisper the secret in my ear
Let me join your circle around the fire
I've been stashed away beneath a floorboard
Hearing muffled voices from above
I always pretend I know what they're saying

Society's Fleeting Glow

by Meilin Storm

My hands shook as I held onto the blue screen,
Attached to people I've never seen.
A window to all that I knew, all I'd deem.

The city's dull and lifeless gray,
Lit only by pixels that carried the day.
Had the blue light stolen the sun?
When was the last time I'd spoken to someone?

Fingers twitched, but never to touch
Only to scroll, to tap, to waste.
A sitcom laughed from a television light,
But no one listened,
Instead, being met with downward stares.

And as I looked up, just for a breath,
I saw my family, silent as death.
Faces lit not by warmth nor grace,
But by a glow that replaced their space.
We exist together, yet remain alone.
Suffocated in a world where we've never been.

Privileged

by Kloe Bryant

As the sun begins to sets
I roll into my bed
I reach for my phone
And I scroll and scroll
To the point my thumb begins to fall off
My eyes search through the heated headlines
The suggested social media posts
And part of me can't help but want to cry
And then, a sense of realization of how privileged I am rushes over me
I'm white.
I have a roof over my head.
I have people providing what they can for me.
I may not be able to afford the same clothes my friends do
Or the 8-dollar Starbucks cold brew
And I may be less privileged than my peers
But I'm privileged enough to realize I'm privileged.

Social Media Arch

by Bella DeCarli

One scroll leads to one hour of constant dopamine One laugh leads to two hours of scrolling One video leads to three hours of TikTok Sitting, lying, or even walking
Constant reinforcement
Constant dopamine rushes
Constant happiness
Creating unhealthy behaviors
Impatient
Angry
Annoyed
Stubborn
The long days
The hard day
Grab your phone
Click an app
Scroll until your eyes droop
No thoughts
No worries
Just the scroll
Happy video
Funny video
Sad video
Scary video
All give a rush
A feeling that people yearn for
Social media
Drags and pulls
Without you even realizing

Distractions

by Juniper Otter

I've been sad for a while,
Been a bit since I've seen a completely sunny day,
I think you understand

Missed the mark for perfect by a mile,
Listen to music to keep the demons at bay,
I think you understand,

I watch a Disney cartoon, and the villain's obvious, full of guile,
I point at them, "They're the one to blame," I say,
I think you understand,

An easy solution to halt the spew of bile,
And the heroes put the villain away,
I think you understand,

Well, *do* you understand?

The world is a scary, scary place,
And my body and my voice are always under threat,
There's no singular villain,
No easy solution wrapped with a neat bow,

So I grab the joy I can,
Hold it tight enough near to bursting,
(It's called POP culture for a reason),
Because by all that we hold dear,
We have got to stay afloat,

And so we stay afloat,
Don't rock the boat,
I think you understand,

Whiskey tears, beers,
Cigarettes, vapes, get your poison here,

Drink down those warehouses full,
Of ready-made clothing ready,
To fall apart,
Sip the Stanley cup,
Stanley parable,

Gulp the water, or part it like Moses,
(If you're religiously inclined),

Protest, march,
The police march over the bodies of,
Black men, Black women, Black kids, Black Lives Matter,
Do you understand?

But wait-
This isn't the right kind of escape!

Religious revival,
Thump that Bible,
Drink the wine,
Drink the gospel,
Eat the Man alive,

Argue, Brawl,
Anything at all,
To cloud the mind,
And pay no mind,
As the dam gets closer to fracture,
Do you understand?

Pop culture reflects the time,
Reflects our mind,
Our shows have gotten darker,
The woes have gotten sharper,
I think you understand,

Queer kids are on television,
And women are leading revolutions,
But at the same time,
Our laws are regressing,
Do you understand?

It's a veritably unbearable pushmi-pullyu,
And the only way to halt the tug-tug-tug,
Is to submit to the drudgery of change,
Because escape is sweet,
But it's sweeter to never need escape at all,

Do you understand?

Human

by Greg Pronovost-Carlson

They told me that I was too fat

"when you walk around the stage in a black bikini in front of millions of viewers, people are going to notice" (CBS).

"The bulging belly she was flaunting was SO not hot" (CBS).

And they told me that my nose made me a villain

Gargamel, Mother Gothel, Lady Tremaine, Ursula, Gaston, Hades, the list goes on.

And they told me my religion makes me a terrorist

"white people are never terrorists." (Corbin)

"Muslim terrorist." (Corbin)

And they told me my sexuality makes me a predator

"Groomer"

"Child predator"

"historical prejudice and stigma have depicted LGBTQ people—especially gay/bisexual men—as sexual predators." (Loyal)

And they told me I could never be good enough because of my disability

"Perhaps the most common stereotype of persons with disabilities is the victim, a character who is presented as a helpless object of pity or sympathy." (MediaSmarts)

"The flip side of the victim stereotype is the hero, the character who proves her worth by overcoming her disability." "It makes audiences feel better about the condition of persons with a disability without having to accommodate them, reinforcing the notion that disability can be overcome if only the person would "try hard enough"" (MediaSmarts)

And they told me my gender made me mentally ill

"The DSM considered being transgender a mental illness until 2013" "God can fix you"

And I thought to myself, *doctors also thought that cocaine and cigarettes fixed everything once, does that make it true?*

And they told me that my language made me an "alien"

"U.S. citizens still view Spanish through a lens of suspicion and disdain." (NBC)

"English is our first language, so you need to speak English. Get the f--- out of my country." (NBC)

"Hispanics should work harder at assimilation." (NBC)

And they told me that my race made me inferior

"boy"

"redlining" (Gross)

"we are accused of racism against white people, and the avoidance of accountability continues." (Eddo-Lodge)

Love Canal, Niagara Falls

"second-class citizens" (Gross)

"African American women were not taken as seriously as those of the working-class white women, due largely to institutionalized racism and misunderstandings based on class differences." (Gross)

And they told me that my tattoos made me a criminal

Nobody will ever hire you with all those tattoos

"philosophers related tattoos to people's economic, and racial status. They found that the people who had tattoos were lower-class citizens who have been to jail." (Bona Venture)

And they tell me my accent makes me sound undereducated or "funny"

"You must be so *smart* to have learned English and to be *so fluent*"

"Deeming someone as "less truthful" (...) due to their accent" (Ivy Exec)

"Considering someone unqualified or assuming they lack credibility due to their accent" (Ivy Exec)

And they tell me my country is poor when it's they who exploit us

"The DRC is rich in natural resources, including coltan, gold, diamonds and cobalt. The exploitation of these minerals is a significant driver of prolonged conflicts" (Amnesty)

"The conflicts in the DRC have ignited a human rights catastrophe. Thousands of civilians are caught in the crossfire and sexual violence is rampant. War crimes and crimes against humanity have been documented. Those who survive the violence face mass displacement, hunger, disease and poverty." (Amnesty)

And they tell me I should just give up on my kid because they're "different"

"Stop Saying You're Sorry That My Daughter is Disabled" (Frances)

"Stop telling parents of disabled children how strong they are or "I can't imagine how you do it."" (Frances)

"She is a kid, just like any other kid, who loves to have the same experiences as other children. The only difference is that most of those experiences are not accessible to her." (Frances)

And they say I'm too white to be Black but too (...) to be (...) and too (..) to be (...)

"What Are You?" (Robbins)

"Are you even Bangladeshi? You're too white to be a true Bangladeshi." (Robbins)

"it is professedly dormant for people to assume that identity can be summed up in one word: Black, white, Latinx, Jewish, Muslim, Bangladeshi, American, etc. The concept of identity is much more complex than that." (Robbins)

They tell me there's nothing they can do for me and yet they don't even try

"Overall, women experience more chronic pain than men. Despite this (...) medical professionals are more likely to dismiss women patients as too sensitive, hysterical, or as time-wasters." (Medical News)

"62% of people with an autoimmune disease had been labeled "chronic complainers" by doctors," "However, 75% of people with autoimmune conditions are women." (Medical News)

He says, she says, they say, we say, I say, you say, but I am…

But you are…

But we are
But he is
But she is
But they are

Human.

…And yet, they tell me I should change…

Works Cited

Corbin, Caroline Mala. "Terrorists Are Always Muslim but Never White: At the Intersection of Critical Race Theory and Propaganda." *FLASH: The Fordham Law Archive of Scholarship and History*.

thisisloyal.com, Loyal |. "LGBTQ People on Sex Offender Registries in the US." *Williams Institute*, 7 July 2022.

"Common Portrayals of Persons with Disabilities." *MediaSmarts*.

"How the U.S. Taught Me That Spanish Was Shameful." *NBCNews.com*, NBCUniversal News Group, 26 Mar. 2019.

Gross, Terry. "A 'forgotten History' of How the U.S. Government Segregated America." *NPR*, 3 May 2017.

Eddo-Lodge, Reni. "Why I'm No Longer Talking to White People about Race." *The Guardian*, Guardian News and Media, 30 May 2017.

"People Are Not Defined by Their Tattoos." *The Bona Venture*, 2 Apr. 2021.

"What Is Accent Discrimination, and How Can You Prevent It in the Workplace?" *Ivy Exec*, 28 Sept., 2023.

"Why Is the Democratic Republic of Congo Wracked by Conflict?" *Amnesty International*, 5 Nov. 2024.

Frances Pimentel, and Frances Pimentel. "Stop Saying You're Sorry That My Daughter Is Disabled- +4 Other Things I Wish You Knew as a Parent of a Child with Disabilities." *Milk Drunk*, 13 Nov. 2023.

Robbins, Denise. "'What Are You?' - How Struggles with Multiculturalism Have Informed My Activism." *Chesapeake Climate Action Network*, 28 July 2020.

"Gender Bias in Medical Diagnosis: Facts, Causes, and Impact." *Medical News Today*, MediLexicon International.

The Generation of Magpies

by Fiona Smart

Shiny objects in the distance,

Attracting magpies and their mimicking existence. Curious yet hoarding traits,

The magpies fail to be in isolated states. Constantly searching for something shiny, However the significance could be quite tiny. Is it even known…

Why they search for used chrome?

The magpies all look the same,

Black and white feathers, a consistent domain. "Stealers of things",

He endlessly sings.

Feening for more, a something without purpose The magpies hit and scratch the surface. Scavenging the circuits of their entrapments, They rummage and collect indiscriminate fragments. Unoriginal passions not sourced from the head But stolen from the veins of those who bled. What point does it all combine…

When trends influence and drain the mind? What does it pitch…

The great Internet itch?

Perpetual flows of evident fads;

A disposable interest, it only adds.

For the magpies clench to certain mentalities,

Habitually full of blatant banalities.

The shiny objects in the distance,

Are microtrends of insignificance.

Buttons, coins, rings, and keys:

The fortune that always seems to please. Today's trinkets outweigh the treasures, Filling the nest with temporary pleasures Soon the paint washes away

Revealing a cheap plastic decay.

They confuse the treasures with a deceptive match Forced to scour again from scratch.

Overwhelmed by the constant churning The magpies search to fulfill their yearning. A generation of magpies, so it breeds,

"Stealers of things", that nobody needs.

High School Graduation

by Dulce Ramos

I might take a gap year.
That's something I'm preparing to say when senior graduation comes.
Three months and twenty-eight days until we walk up that stage, glistening in the sun,
In our caps and gowns of solid night that we procrastinated to buy until the very last second.
It's probably just the senioritis kicking in,
Stealing the will to keep going on with tests and multiple-part math questions
That should take 30 minutes to finish but instead takes me 30 minutes to begin
Taking away hours of sleepless nights that got me to a place higher than what really should've been.
I don't know if you can tell, but I'm not exactly your average dairy drink
you pick up during lunch, cramming your way through a line that's on the brink
Of turning into a riot of hungry teens faster than you can blink.
Instead I'm basically everyone's favorite, chocolate milk.
A proud, full-blooded Mexican
Born from the roots of a Oaxacan and Sinaloan
That have bid their families goodbye and sneak into a world with promises of doors that are always open.
California.
The place of diversity and way too expensive housing, the place they first met
And where they planted their new home for the future 3 children they have yet
To bring into the world, their fate now set.
An unknown amount of years later, they had me.
A shrimp-sized baby

With newly squinting eyes, ready to see
And already holding so much responsibility.
A responsibility to make a life here in America that my parents were meant to,
The land of equality!
I mean just take a look at our school!
An entire class to teach students "¡Hola! ¿Como estas? Bien, ¿y tu?"
The beautiful language of Spanish meant for you,
As Chicano students back in the day couldn't even speak their native tongue or else they'd face getting beaten by a wooden paddle until their asses were painted blue.
But hey, I'm glad to hear people sharing how to say cat or 3 sentence chats in Español -
Oops! *Don't tell my teacher I said that.*
They added Spanish for Native/Heritage Speakers in 2023
An extraordinary class with a wonderful teacher to help us be
One with our cultura, our musica, and figuras importantes in our history
While also handing out Caregiver's Authorization Affidavit forms during the beginning of class like your typical homework assignment, though they'd never agree,
 in case I.C.E. officers come in the middle of the night and take my parents away from me.
America, the land of giving!
The land of opportunity, to make a living
Just make sure to read the fine print on the right corner of your birth certificate that you receive
Stating, "Only applies to people who are straight, white, male, and wealthy".
Where is the giving?
Because throughout all my life and my parent's life and my Spanish teacher's life and every Single Mexican American, born or not born on U.S. soil's life has only seen you take.

You take our language for white kids to learn when they're barely even fluent in their own.

You take our food as if it's a mascot for your multi-millionaire fast food chain restaurants while Mexican immigrants barely have enough money to afford a chicken bone,

Those same ingredients being used created by the muddied hands that never slow

You take children's parents and family who just wanted a future in a land that is now a warzone

Because you don't want dirt in your home.

But thank fucking god you give me the privilege of joining them however you see fit

Like the 14th Amendment never existed

And constantly make me fear you'll take my right to go to college next before I get the chance to even be enlisted.

17 years, 10 months, and 10 days is how long I've worked to reach that goal,

And you could take it away in 2 months and 28 days.

So now, I have to practice what to say

When people come up to me and ask, "So, what'll you do after you graduate?"

And I will be prepared to state,

"I don't know, I might take a gap year."

Echoes of the Night Before
(After Hadestown)

by Autumn Hudgens

Night air hangs heavy
with echoes of ancient tragedy drifting through stars
like leaves lost in a winter breeze,
a new generation humming an old melody with hope of a better ending. The
story: A dreamer. A seeker. The love in between.
Orpheus & Eurydice.
In this version poet boy meets poor girl looking for something to eat.
Teaches her how to dream, how to live.
Lights up her world with wonder before winter blows in,
before doubt drags them apart,
love pulling like a magnet against the strength of insecurity to
give false hope before
he turns to see her face &
the final curtain closes
on our prayers.

Notes of this lost melody linger in the auditorium as silhouettes stand onstage,
closing the gap between myth & reality as they wait
for this story to end, for the next to begin. For
the next cue. The next
line. The next song.
Friends & friends of friends & enemies of friends
don masks for the night to look back at the way things used to be,
become echoes of the past & muses of the future.

Tonight, under the spotlights, they are our muses
as lovely voices weave ancient tapestries with

words far more graceful than the thoughts that run through my head, my
own myth coming to life,
hidden between the notes where no one
can find them but me.
The story: A dreamer. A seeker. The distance between.
This time the dreamer is no son of a muse, instead
daughter of daughters who brought her
somewhere she could fulfill all their dreams for her.
This time the seeker no longer seeks a meal & warmth,
instead fights through every storm to find
her own road to follow to a life worth living, for her own way to
bring the world back into tune.
In this version girl meets girl & they teach each other
how to succeed. How to keep walking any road
in spite of the storm, the hunger, the cold.
Dreamer shows seeker a new way to see the world,
how her passion & drive brighten the darkest nights, keep
them warm through the coldest winds, how she
has become the summer sun.
Seeker shows dreamer how her song
is more precious than she could have imagined,
how it makes obstacles come to life to let her pass.
For a moment,
the dreamer dares to dream of a world where she speaks out for herself. For a
moment, she looks to the future
instead of the past.

But like seasons, winds can change,
& the confidence of a confidant can only go so far
when doubt creeps into the mind, its shadows
closing in on logic like a curtain.

Only the sunlight of summer keeps these
shadows at bay.

The story: The dreamer, lost in her head.
                The seeker, exhausted on the stage.
                The distance between myth & reality indistinguishable
from the distance between seats & stage,
it is all a matter of perspective.
In this version the story is still unfinished,
songs still unsung echoing through the space between
the seeker & the dreamer.
They know the journey home is the hardest one
to traverse alone.
The promise to keep moving forward the most difficult to keep.
There is never truly an end.
Legend echoes itself through time & take,
weaves itself into every fiber of our being.
Repeats itself in every new story.
It promises
that the dreamer will always look back one more time,
for better or for worse.
Yet we still hope it will turn out differently.

The Purpose of Music

by Peyton Ellis Studebaker

I am on the bus, coming home from school,
I slide my slick, black Samsung headphones,
Pressing the cushions over my ears,
When I press play the world fades around me.
The music swells in time with my heart,
My lungs and airways are filled with the delicious scent of pure emotion.
I soon get lost in the feeling of sweet symphonies and delicate dissonance.

Every genre of this exquisite noise takes me places,
Pulling me along with soft hands and eager smiles,
I let it take the lead.
When I listen to Alex G I feel peaceful,
I am sent to beautiful grassy hills, littered with flowers and ladybugs,
The feeling of sunlight on my face and the sweet scent of spring right around the corner,
fluffy clouds shaped particularly and hung in the baby blue sky by mother nature herself.
When I listen to Mitski I feel cold,
Lonely, trudging through the aftermath of a winter snow in the dark of night,
My socks soaked through with slush from the roads
The words feel like frost biting at my skin,
And when I look up there are no stars, not even the mercy of light from the moon.

As we travel the world and beyond,
Skimming through every mind of every creator:
Sometimes the mind is somber, and it feels trapped and grey,
Sometimes the mind thrilling, vibrant colors swirl;
Along with scents of fruits and hope.
Sometimes the mind is angry, the smell smoke and feeling the heat of betrayal
Sometimes the words roll sharp in the artist's mouth

And sometimes the words are soft,
Comforting like a down blanket

Through this music my eyes can finally open,
I am able to experience many different stories,
To understand.
I keep them close to my heart and take in every emotion;
The sound of the oppressed,
the wailing of a lost lover,
or even the smooth feel of a sunny day

Through this music I feel connected,
With myself as well as the targeted audience.
And I feel seen.
I look myself in the mirror and know that there are others that I share with,
Similar stories and feelings all come together to form the human race,
And I am in the center.

Thin to Win

by Lilian Mion

First thing in the morning, opening the first social media app I see
Caption: What I eat in a Day to Stay Skinny

I was about to make breakfast
I cuff my pointer and thumb around my wrist

I put the bagel I was about to eat away
I look in the mirror. "Why do I look like this?" "I can't live this way."

"I need to change."
Hopefully, enough to drop 10 pounds by summer, or I'll be deranged

Day by day, less on my plate
Week after week, I lost weight

I'm filled with sorrow
Struggling to make it to tomorrow

I was nothing but a skeleton frame
Constantly filled with shame

Starving myself to fit in
My eyes went black, what a life this has been

I woke up surrounded by nurses rushing my mom, who was crying in the hospital chair
All of this to look like the girls on my phone, it is so unfair

Short Story

The Last Pearl

by Elizabeth Gibbons

Avis slowly opened her eyes. For a moment she could not remember where she was. Then it all came flooding back to her. The dragons were going to destroy the school if they didn't get their eggs back. They had to find the last pearl today. They had already found the first three pearls at the Golden Gate Bridge, Mount Rushmore and the Space Needle. They were guarded by the four directions, a group of animals from Chinese mythology. The last pearl was guarded by the Azure Dragon at the Statue of Liberty. It was nestled inside the torch. Visitors were no longer allowed to climb up to the torch because Battery Park didn't want mortals finding the pearl. Also the statue is 305 feet tall. And the torch is higher. And they had to get it. How?

"You up yet Avis?" said her twin sister Lupine. Lupine was tall with black hair that went down to her waist and eyes the color of hazel. They looked like copies of each other. Sometimes they tricked the teachers at Moonstone Academy by saying that Lupine was Avis and Avis was Lupine. It was great fun to see the looks on their faces.

"Nearly." said Avis. She noticed that Atlanta was also getting up. Like her and Lupine, Atlanta also had hazel eyes but her hair was the color of hot chocolate and she liked to wear it in different hairstyles. She was normally very quiet but don't underestimate her...unless you want to jump in a lake. Just ask Xia.

Just then the door opened. They were staying at the Emerald Staff, the biggest magical hotel in North America. The Emerald Staff was invisible to mortals. It was a huge marble building with The Emerald Staff written in green cursive at the top. How they got their reservation was all due to their familiars. And speaking of familiars...

"Good, you're up." said Vesta. Vesta was Avis' familiar. Also she was a phoenix. She was just how you would expect a phoenix to look. Her feathers were red and gold and her eyes were a deep blue,the color of the ocean. Reika, Lupine's familiar, was a wolf. Her fur was sliver, like the caves at the Lost Coast. Diana, Atlanta's familiar was a lynx. She was all brown with black spots. Avis liked to say that they were familiars because Atlanta's hair was the same color as Diana's fur. "Got everything?" asked Reika. "Yep" said Avis.

"Make sure you have the pearls." said Atlanta. Diana nodded. She opened her backpack which was a deep blue. In it was her room key, the compass, the latest edition of the Sorcerer's Times which she has picked up last night, and of course the red embroidered bag which held the pearls. My amulet! She thought in a panic. Her hands went to her throat. It was sitting around her neck, just as it had been since the fateful day. Nine months ago her, Atlanta, Lupine, and their familiars were teleported to the Owl Abode of North America's headquarters and given these amulets which allowed them to control water.

Every century or two, The Owl Abode chooses three magical kids to be the new owners of these amulets which allows the wearer to be able to control a part of the elements. The ones that Avis, Lupine and Atlanta had are the water ones. Wizards in North America mostly travel by cloud. Avis was jerked out of her reverie by Lupine saying "Come on Avis, stop daydreaming and let's get some breakfast." She shook herself out of her stupor and turned to follow the rest of the group out of the door. Earlier she had changed into a dark green Moonstone Academy shirt and jeans. The others were wearing similar outfits to that. They came to a circle of doors which had letters at the top of them. To access the clouds they had to swipe the room key on the screen and say where you wanted to go. "Room key, anybody have a room key?" said Reika Lupine took hers out of her pocket. Reika swiped it with her paw against the screen. Green letters started to form. Where would you like to go? it read. "Topaz Restaurant." said Reika. The screen said Take Cloud B to Topaz Restaurant. One of the many doors around them opened. They could see the cloud waiting for them, but if they took too long the cloud would leave without them.

"Quick, hurry before it leaves." said Diana. They all ran onto the cloud. There was white seats in a circle on the cloud. Their hotel room was on the 30th floor. At the Emerald Staff they didn't have elevators they had clouds, but nobody fell off because they had a magical barrier around them. A couple minutes later they were at the Topaz Restaurant and feasting on a meal of bagels and eggs. Lupine took a big bite of her Everything Bagel when she suddenly thought of a problem. "Don't you need tickets to go to the top?" she wondered aloud.

"Vesta has apparently got a plan." said Diana. Avis turned to look at Vesta. She winked. When all of them were done with their food, they went over to the gondola station. It was on the same floor as the restaurant. Gondolas are the normal type of gondola, but mortals see them as clouds. They let wizards travel all over the world. Twenty minutes later they were sailing over New York in a gondola. They could see all the buildings spread out below them.

"We have arrived." said Lupine. They had landed at Battery Park in the highest branch of a pine tree. It looked exactly how they imagined. They paid the driver ten drachmas and got out. The gondola closed its doors and sped off over all the skyscrapers. They climbed down from the pine tree and looked around.

"Where do we go?" asked Diana. Avis had spotted the signs with the Statue of Liberty on them. A big crowd of people seemed to be heading that way. It was probably the right way to go to get to the ferry. Avis said this to Vesta who thought it was a good idea. So they followed the immense crowd of People.

"That's probably the right place to go" said Vesta. She gestured to a huge brown archway with her right wing that said Clinton Castle on it. They walked through it and saw the ticket inspector's booth. "Who's handling her?" asked Atlanta, jabbing a finger toward the ticket inspector. "Allow me" said Vesta. She spread her wings and flew over to the ticket inspector's booth. Avis Lupine and Atlanta looked at each other. "She has always been daring" said Avis. They glanced at Vesta. Everyone ran after her. When they finally caught up with Vesta, they heard her having a conversation with the lady at the booth.

"Excuse me, how can I help you?" asked the lady. She looked very businesslike with her brown hair tied back in a bun. Lupine whispered to Avis "Her and Xia would get along perfect". Avis had to agree. Xia was very businesslike. Also snobbish. "We have six tickets for the crown." said Vesta. She handed them through the slot in the booth. Avis, Lupine and Atlanta shot confused looks at each other. Where had Vesta managed to get tickets? The lady handed them wristbands and official tickets. Vesta handed them to Reika who handed them to Diana.

"I'd move if I were you," said the lady, "You don't want to wait thirty minutes for another ferry to come, the ferry currently boarding right now leaves in ten minutes, good bye and have a nice time visiting The Statue of Liberty." They thanked her and ran off to the dock where orange-vested security guards were shepherding people onto the boat. A couple minutes later they were on the ferry. "Statue of Liberty here we come!" said Atlanta. Avis sat down and opened her backpack. She had done a little mind magic on those security guards to have them allow her to take her backpack to the Statue of Liberty. She looked out of the window. If she looked hard enough, she could see the Statue of Liberty holding its torch high in the air. And the pearl is somewhere in there, thought Avis. Avis turned to Vesta and asked, "Where did you get crown tickets?"

"Oh they were not really tickets at all, they were just blank pieces of paper." said Vesta, "Mortals are just oblivious." Avis laughed. "We're here." said Lupine. Avis looked out of the window. She could see the Statue of Liberty towering above them.

"Breathtaking, isn't it?" asked Atlanta. Avis agreed. They joined the crowd getting off the boat. Five minutes later they were climbing the narrow staircase to the top of the statue. "So many stairs" huffed Atlanta.

"My feet haven't been this tired since we almost got tagged in the Talisman game" said Lupine. "Couldn't you have just flown us up there?" said Avis to Vesta, who was circling above their heads. Phoenixes can carry heavy loads. "The mortals would've gotten suspicious." "It's all right for you, you're a BIRD" said Lupine. Vesta changed tack at the speed of light. She also looked a bit sheepish.

"Oh look we're at the top of the pedestal. Do you want to stop and look out?" They went onto the pedestal where they could see the whole glittering metropolis of New York. Avis thought that the view from the pedestal was amazing. Lupine and Atlanta clearly felt the same way. They went back inside the statue and saw an orange sign with the Statue of Liberty on it. "146 steps to the top" groaned Atlanta. "And I'm so looking forward to it. Not." 146 steps later they were at the top of the statue. They were in a very narrow space in the crown. If they looked out of the window they could see the slate that said July IV MDCCLXXIV, the date when the Declaration of Independence was signed.

"It is unbelievably tiny in here." said Reika. She was right. It was very squished at the top. "Um" said Lupine, "does anyone realize that we're alone up here?" Avis looked around. "Now that you mention it" said Avis "There is nobody up here." "That security guard just appeared out of nowhere." said Atlanta. Diana suddenly backed into the fifth glass window "We should go." she said. "Yes, we should go." said Reika. "That's a good idea." said Vesta. "What is happening with you guys?" said Avis. She glanced at the security guard. She smiled at her. Flames flickered in and out of her mouth. Wait, flames? She turned to Lupine and Atlanta to say this but found they had already noticed it. Lupine was eyeing the stairs as if she was going to run down them at a moment's notice. The security guard stood up. She slowly transformed into a pure white dragon. She snarled then jumped right at them.

"WAIT!!" screamed Reika, her wolf ears were down and she looked a bit nervous, but her voice was steady. The dragon froze in mid jump. "What?" asked the dragon. Her voice was ancient. It reminded Avis of those Redwood trees at Moonstone Academy. "We just want the pearl." said Vesta. "Call me Azure" she said. "You don't seem like evil people, so you can have the pearl." While she was saying this she was walking up another staircase, this time to the torch. Everyone followed her up the staircase. "I live inside the flame of the torch. Bartholdi built it for me personally, I rather liked it when they covered the flame in twenty-four karat gold, and I remember when the hand and torch was exhibited in Philadelphia for the World's Fair.

"But that was in 1876. How old are you?" asked Lupine who was examining the intricate patterns on the inside of the torch that Azure had probably carved herself. She certainly had claws sharp enough for the job.

"That I will never tell" said Azure. "And yes, you can take the pearl" she added, handing a sky blue pearl to Avis. Avis put it in her backpack. "It will just come back to me anyway, after you ask your Question."

"Do you happen to have any drachmas?" asked Atlanta "We spent all of ours on Gondola fare." Azure dropped a couple of them in Atlanta's outstretched hand. "You could get a gondola back instead of more stairs" suggested Azure. "I can summon one." "That is the best thing you ever said!" said Atlanta. A couple of minutes later they were speeding off in one of the gondolas, heading back to the Emerald Staff. "When do you think we should try the pearls?" asked Lupine.

"Maybe when we're back at the hotel." said Atlanta. "Guys we're here." said Avis. They stepped out of the gondola. Atlanta paid the driver ten drachmas and it sped off. They opened the door and walked over to the clouds. Lupine took out her room key and swiped it on the screen. She said Floor 30 room 25 when the screen asked Where do you want to go? One of the doors opened. They hurried onto the cloud. A couple minutes later they were in the hotel room.

Atlanta was pacing around and around. "What if it doesn't work?" she wondered. Avis, Lupine and Atlanta put the four sky blue pearls in the holes in the black compass. They started to spin. And then they levitated up. "Ask the question, ask the question" said Vesta, all insistent. Avis nervously asked, "Where are the dragon eggs?" The pearls merged together to form one big pearl about a foot and a half tall. It started to show a vision. "No I don't believe it" said Avis.

"This is horrifying" said Lupine. "I saw that place" said Atlanta, "That's Cleopatra's Needle!!!"

TO BE CONTINUED...

Andrew's Rise of Soccer

by Wilhelmina Luna

Soccer is a great sport. Andrew is 14 and likes soccer, but he's not that good at it. Jimmy and his friends bully Andrew at school and online because he's bad at soccer. Andrew has one good friend, Jason. Jimmy's rich and spoiled so he gets what he wants. His parents have been paying $2,000 a lesson for him to be the best at soccer since he was 8. Andrew's family doesn't have that kind of money so he has to figure out how to get good at soccer on his own.

Andrew decides he is going to search soccer lessons on social media. He follows a famous soccer player and works every day to copy his moves. One month later, it's soccer season and Andrew wants to join the soccer team, but he doesn't want to be around Jimmy so he doesn't join. He doesn't play but he watches every one of their games, avoiding Jimmy.

Andrew was at a soccer game and Jimmy tripped and sprained his ankle. When Jimmy sprained his ankle the team was down a player. The coach asked if Andrew wanted to play, and Andrew said yes. When Andrew played he scored 4 goals. He played the rest of the season and won MVP of the year.

He played in the rest of high school and college and then he got drafted to a professional soccer team in a whole other country. He is one of the best soccer players in the world now. He is now playing soccer and traveling all over the world.

Andrew was motivated by a professional soccer player that he would not have been able to learn from if it wasn't for social media. Social media can give you opportunities you would not normally have that help you be successful and happy if you use it right.

We Don't Care

by June Wickman

One day when me and my besties Allison and Averil were window shopping at the mall we stopped to go into Daiso. The music in there was poppin so we started dancing and goofing around. It was really fun! After a little while of us having fun and dancing a girl comes up to us and gives us a weird look (she was about our age).

We all made the decision to go up to her and make her understand what we think! We walked up to her and told her that we don't care what she thinks of us, and that she is probably just jealous that we were having fun. Then we walked away and started goofing around, because why not!

After all of that we decided to go to a restaurant in the mall. We all had a long conversation about that girl. My friend mentioned how she thinks that pop culture really makes people judgmental! I totally agreed with her, but I also think that it is important to remember that pop culture makes some people more confident like me and my besties. Me, Avral, and Alison laughed the whole rest of the day about it!

Reflections

by Symon Mendoza

Monday mornings were always drab. My body ached with exhaustion, the clock ticking menacingly as school lingered in the near future. But alas, it was a necessary part of my life, so I found joy in the routine.

I pulled myself out of bed and strolled to the poorly lit bathroom. There, I faced the large mirror and brushed my morning breath away. While doing so, I examined my reflection, analyzing the features plastered to her face. Her brown curls fell loose and wild, covering her chubby cheeks and clean skin. I smiled at the girl in my mirror, and she smiled back. I loved seeing her; she was beautiful. Truly beautiful.

School sped by fast that day. One minute I was learning fractions, the next I was stepping off the afternoon bus and running back home. Bursting through the front door was like a fresh breath of springtime air, after the hideous rain had shied away. Oh how I bathed in it. I flopped down on the couch, feeling myself sink into the stiff cushions.

But, as I sat there, I began to feel something creep up on me. Something which sucked away my energy as a vampire sucks blood. Something that made time feel frozen, unmoving. It was that nasty, dreaded feeling of boredom.

I groaned, feeling stuck as another minute passed disguised as an hour. As I sat there, counting seconds, I suddenly remembered an app my friends told me about. TikTok! I wasn't quite sure what it was, but if they all liked it, I should too. I swiftly picked up my phone and downloaded TikTok.

Some may wonder what exactly TikTok was. Scrolling. That's what the app was. You'd scroll through an endless amount of 15 second videos. Saying it now makes the app sound as interesting as watching concrete harden, but to my ten-year old self, this app was transcendent. I could see millions of people in the span of seconds, and even better, I could feel them. It was as if the people were sitting at my side.

They weren't talking to a screen, they were talking to me! With millions right next to me, I would never be alone.

For days, I'd scroll on that app, consuming whatever content was fed to me. Seldom did I ever stop, and when I did, The app never left my deepest thoughts. It became more and more infrequent for me to leave that app alone. Why would I ever? The app was harmless fun made for some quick dopamine.

So, I kept scrolling. "I'm trash!" The girl on my screen joked. It was a simple sentence, but I laughed at it so hard my head should have launched off my body.

The next day, I repeated that joke to all my friends at school. They all chuckled at it the same way I had. It gave me warmth to hear them laugh. To hear their happiness was to feel their happiness. To hear their love was to feel their love. I couldn't get enough of it.

Back home, I sat on the couch, phone in hand as I mindlessly scrolled. As I went through the videos, I started to notice a pattern. Influencers. Pretty, porcelain influencers. They were beloved, worshipped. And with these influencers, I started to notice a pattern within a pattern.

Each handcrafted individual who appeared to me was perfect. Prettier than a bush of pink roses, the blossoms vibrant, the leaves rich. I yearned to be that. I yearned to be a bush of pink roses. I yearned for the vibrant blossoms and rich leaves. If I could, I would have snipped the flowers right off those influencers and sewed them onto me. And as I saw beautiful girl after beautiful girl, I thought to myself.

"I'm trash."

It should have ended at school. The joke should have disintegrated into dust and blown out of my head. But It didn't. Perhaps that app had melted my brain into slime, disgusting, sticky slime picking up whatever touched its surface. And as the influencers and jokes mixed deeper into my melted mind, a new feeling was born.

Hunger.

In a fit of rage, I threw my phone down on the couch and pondered about my situation. I wanted to be like those influencers right? Pretty perfect porcelain? Well, how could I achieve that? How could I become the rose bushes they were?

What if I used makeup! That's a way to become pretty, right?

So, I tried makeup. I got a sparkly pink eyeshadow pallet and some brushes. Vigorously, I brushed the eyeshadow over my whole eye. When my mom saw my masterpiece, she laughed, saying "you have pink eye!" Clearly, this wasn't the way to become pretty.

After I thought some more, I came to a new solution: dieting. I could diet! Of course! That was much easier than makeup. I first tried eating as little as possible, sticking to salads and such, but I couldn't last a day. The fridge called to me like a lustful siren, and me, the gluttonous sailor, swam right to it.

Defeated, I lay on my bedroom floor, feeling the shaggy carpet below my fingers. Outside, rain knocked on the window, while gusts of wind accompanied it in a low hum. It was peaceful, to lay there in my dimly lit room. But the peace was killed by a deep sinking feeling that drowned me in despair.

I was a failure. I couldn't set a goal and stick to it for one day. Not even to be perfect porcelain like the influencers I surrounded myself with. I was nothing but cheap plastic. Cheap ugly plastic.

Pathetic.

With a sigh, I pulled myself up and wandered to the bathroom. There, I slowly opened the door and stepped inside. The scent of sweet, rosy soap greeted me, despite the mess of various scattered objects in place. Turning on the light, I slowly walked over to the mirror.

I raised my head to look in the reflection and noticed something terrible looking back into my eyes. Myself. She was ugly. Her face was fatty, her hair was frizzy, her skin was like that of a snake. She was worse than just an unattractive girl, she was trash. Filthy, disgusting trash.

I sprinted out of the bathroom, shutting the door behind me with a slam. I wanted to keep her trapped in that bathroom, keep her away from me at all costs. Standing in the hallway, I desperately looked for a distraction, something to take me out of this disgusting reality. I turned my head to the little green couch, spotting my phone laying on it ever so peacefully. I thought about that app, the one that led me down this path.

The app spoke to me, beckoning me to open it and scroll. It called to me like a spinning wheel, if I was the princess doomed to prick her finger and fall beneath its curse. In my mind, somewhere deep in my mind, I knew that this app would kill me, bury my soul and take its place. But, despite this grueling knowledge, I plopped down on the couch and began scrolling.

Video after video, women were praised or degraded for their looks. Value was based on the face, the body, the presence. People decided one was more adequate than the other because one was pretty. And the pretty one was the opposite of me. Was I not adequate? Did I even matter?

No, not when the standard is looks.

One more video. One more gorgeous porcelain woman praised only for her looks. One more video. One more woman like me calling herself trash. One more video. One more reminder I'll never be beloved for my looks as an influencer. One more video. One more reminder that I'm trash. One more video. One more reminder. Video. Reminder. Video. Reminder!

Until something broke the pattern.

 A girl danced in front of her mirror, brightly smiling as she swung her hips side-to-side. This kind of skit was common, but something about the girl wasn't. She didn't conform to the beauty standard on this app. She wasn't porcelain or perfect, but despite all of this, she flaunted her looks. She showed off what the world told her to hide. She took pride in what she should have been ashamed of. She was confident and happy. She was a bush of pretty pink roses blooming in the sun. She was beautiful.

I turned off my phone, the screen going black as my tired reflection appeared. For a moment, I stared at her, and she stared back at me. There was something odd about the way she looked. It was hard to explain. Nothing physical was to be pointed out, but it seemed the lights in her eyes had flickered away, leaving only a looming darkness. And in the darkness, there was nothing but cold emptiness.

Where had I gone?

Outside, the storm clouds rolled away, sunlight peeking through. Warm air kissed my skin gently as I trotted along the streets. I began to observe those around me, taking note of their features. One person was tall and skinny, while another was fatter with a chubby face. Some people had wrinkles, holding deep wisdom from the past. Some people had scars, memories etched in their physique. Some had freckles. Some had hooked noses. Some had acne. Some had wide smiles. And, though rare, some people had none of these things at all. But no matter who I saw, I noticed something the same in each one. All of them were flawed.

All of them were perfect.

Stopping for a moment, I gazed into a storefront window and examined my reflection. Her face was chubby, but she had the cutest smile. Her hair was messy, but looked delightful when styled and dolled up. Her skin was acne ridden, but it shined in the sunlight as an opal crystal might.

Maybe she wasn't ugly, maybe she wasn't pretty. Maybe, the girl I saw in the reflection didn't need to be. Why would it matter how she looked. Why would it matter when she was happy?

To this day, I still use TikTok. What can I say; scrolling is surprisingly fun! But now, I don't let that app blind me, defining how I see myself. No longer do I let it warp my mirror and my mind. I decide how I see myself, in all the shimmering reflections.

Blue Light

by Eliza Lehman

My scissors cut through the construction paper in a jagged circle. My friends Carina and Madeline sit by me in Art class, talking about summer plans.

"Oh, yeah! I'm going camping, and it's gonna be great," Carina says giddily.

I love camping - feeling like I'm in the olden days, pretending like we just settled in a new land. That's when I had an idea.

I turn to Carina. "Have you ever thought about getting rid of screens...entirely?" I said. She looks at me and smiles, "Actually, yeah, it'd be weird, but sort of cool."
I smirk. "What if we did that?"

Madeline's eyebrows shoot up. "You'd really do that?"

"It'd be like we lived when people didn't have phones to entertain themselves," I continued.

We made some rules. We would only use our phone to communicate with parents. We could only call friends on a landline. We could only watch movies in a theater. Madeline sighs,

"You guys are crazy. You'll give up in the first two weeks."

"Do you want to join us?" Carina asks with a smirk.

She scoffs, "No, that sounds horrible."

"We'll see about that," I say.

Facing Carina, I hold out my hand. "For the entire summer."

We shake on it.

July 1st, 2023

It's about a month into summer, and the no-screen rule's been challenging. Today, I'm hopping on a ten-hour plane ride to Barcelona. However, that's not even the trickiest part.

Without social media other people are watching, I have no idea what "Skibbity Ohio" means.

Being left out is rough. I'm proving Madeline wrong. I will persist.

At the gate, my stepsister pulls out her iPad. My eyes dart from the screen. I've shifted to avoid screens countless times. The airport is full of screens advertising fragrances and vacations.

I can't look anywhere without seeing a glaring screen. Everyone stares into phones, their heads tilted, unaware. My dad, stepmom, brother, step-brother, sister—my whole family are all on screens.

Instead, I grab my book, Anne of Green Gables. My mind creates vivid images of Avonlea and Anne with her red braids and freckles. If I had my phone right now, I'd be scrolling on Instagram finding something strange that draws me in, like somebody showing off how great their summer's going, subconsciously forcing me to compare myself, making me more anxious than I already am waiting for a flight that's becoming delayed, but here I am, reading a book, my mind swirling the words around until they become images. I'm there with Anne, not waiting to board a delayed plane.

I glance at the people still waiting, still looking at their little black boxes. Once aboard the aircraft, I am greeted by kind flight attendants and walk past row after row of screens in seat backs reflecting streaming blue light.

August 20th, 2023

The ocean roars. I'm staring at dune grass; my brother, and dog running in the sand.

My mind is beginning to create a poem; my fingers urge me to write. I know the title already, "Blue Light."

"I don't know it, but it knows everything about me
It is everywhere–
Am I the only person who hasn't
turned into a zombie, walking the earth
not discovering this real world?
A whole world unexplored–
I see people depend on it,
I don't.
There is a way
where you don't have to
look at a blue light."

Tomorrow, I'll be allowed to stare at Instagram and watch shows. After watching everybody rely on their screens, I want to take a cautionary step. I don't want to become addicted to devices like everyone else.

Present day

"In seventh grade, Carina and I didn't use our phones for the entire summer," I said to my new friend, Makena.

"That seems hard," she replied.

I giggle to myself. She has no idea the perspective we gained. We didn't rot our brains binging TV shows. We lived and explored. I created art, adventured with Anne of Green Gables, experienced Europe, took it all in – no shows, no comparison, and no blue light.

"I'd do it again," I said.

Devices distract us from life. I notice people using their phones to escape social interaction. Anytime there's an awkward moment, people pull out their phones instead of pushing through to connect.

Sometimes, when I am excluded from jokes, or feel like an outsider, I feel like maybe life would be better addicted to my device. But then I remember Avonlea, the dunes, conversations with friends, and the entire world, and I know that I will not pay the price of blue light.

Lacy's Blue Summer

by Josephine Maguire

Lacy sat on the toilet, hunched over. She had been stuck in the fetal position for the past half hour. She pressed the palms of her sweaty hands into her lower stomach. It was the second time she had gotten her period, or as her dad called it, her first big step into womanhood. All things related just made her nauseous. She stared at the walls of the bathroom with intense green eyes. Looking at the drywall as if she were searching for something. The paint was a pale baby blue. Brown and white shells lined the perimeter of the mirror. She noticed the spots where toothpaste was splattered over the top of the water faucet. She observed the places where shells were missing and where the glue was peeking through, and attempted to think of anything other than her current situation. The bathroom was part of the laundry room, where she could hear the rhythmic thumping of something heavy and most definitely misplaced in the dryer. Pat was sitting on the kitchen counter, waiting patiently for the cheddar cheese to melt on his tortilla chips. Nachos were his favorite food. His house was two blocks down, but he seemed to practically live with the Anderson family in the summer. Lacy and her brother spent summers with their dad in Pocatello, Idaho.

It was a slow summer's day, just before noon. Everyone was keeping to themselves. Hudson was planted on the couch, reading a comic book. He was snacking on a peanut butter and jelly sandwich. He had just turned 16, and being older than Pat by five years and Lacy by two, he thought he knew everything there was to know about everything.

"Lacy... Lacy... LACY!" Hudson yelled.

"Leave her alone, she is going through some... lady stuff." Pat's voice trailed off.

Hudson looked at him with a blank face. Then he scrunched his nose and continued eating.

"Yuck!"

Pat made his way to the bathroom. The floor creaked under his feet with each step. The house was old and needed work, but Lacy's dad refused to sell it or invest in fixing it. Pat looked with wide eyes at the door and knocked twice. He positioned his right ear against the wooden door, then paused for a second.

"Lacy, are you alright?" Pat said in a sweet and concerned tone.

Lacy felt choked up. It was hard growing up and always having to deal with things alone. Pat was the only person she confided in. He seemed to see her, really see her, more than her family. This being true, there were some things she never talked to anyone about.

"Pat... I need you to run to the liquor store down the street and get..." She didn't finish her sentence, she didn't need to.

"Ok."

Pat grabbed his nachos and walked out the door. Hudson, not giving a single fuck, stayed planted on the couch completely unbothered.

Lacy always bounced between feeling separate from her body and feeling everything all at once. She felt close to her mom, but she really didn't fully trust anyone. So this being the second time she got her period, she felt very vulnerable. She didn't want anyone to know. Vulnerability made her unbearably uncomfortable. She wasn't a very affectionate person either; it wasn't that she didn't love deeply, it just meant her love language was one that kept distance between her and the other person. It took 15 minutes for the tampons to arrive. Her best friend Shasta showed her once how to use a tampon, but it didn't make it much easier. She flushed and then washed her hands in the sink. She made her way to the kitchen to fix up a snack, and they all spent the rest of the day lying around. Breaking the silence for brief moments to complain or ask each other for glasses of water.

The telephone rang and startled Hudson. It was around 8pm in the evening. He picked it up and asked who it was.

"It's Jenny from the Alibi. Your dad had a little too much to drink, so you can't drive, can't you?"

He shot a stern glance at Lacy, a look which made her whole body tense. She glanced back with a look of alexithymia.

"Yes, Ma'am."

He swiped the car keys off the dining room table and rushed out the door. The Alibi was a 20-minute drive. When he arrived, his dad was passed out on the curb.

"Fuck Dad, you can't be doing this," he mumbled.

He dragged his dad's body to the car and buckled him up in the backseat. The car ride was pretty much silent, with the exception of his dad snoring on and off. He pulled in the driveway and had Lacy help walk him in. He fell asleep on the couch that night.

"Pat, now that he's taking up the couch, I can walk you home if you want."

"I'll be just fine, I'll call when I get there," he smiled. However, it couldn't hide his worried look.

Lacy woke up to arguing in the kitchen. It consisted mostly of her dad rambling on about how much of a self-righteous bitch her mom was to her brother.

"You better be careful, Hudson, I say this out of love, you do not want to end up like your mother. A real piece of work that one. I mean, come on, an affair with our neighbor? She could have had some self-respect. You know what's the fucking cherry on top of my day is too?"

Hudson walked out of the kitchen, and he just didn't have the bandwidth; he was fed up with his dad blaming his problems on his mom, who, in reality, was the only one trying to make things right. He hated wrongful blame. Lacy just lay in her bed and stared at the ceiling. The walls were thin, and she heard everything that had been said in that house. Sometimes she would just lay and stare at the ceiling for hours, and just think of nothing. Some nights were worse than others, especially when Chuck was drunk. He didn't hold back then. He never hit Lacy or Hudson, but he was a very, very angry man. He had been ten years sober while married to their mom, and he just couldn't cope after finding out about the cheating. Despite the hangover, the next morning, he was in a better mood, and he knocked on Lacy's door.

"Honey?"

"Yes?"

"Let's go to the movies? Come do something fun with your pops today, alright?"

"Yeah, sure…" She said hesitantly. "Let me get dressed."

 She rolled off her bed and went to her wooden dresser. She was wearing an oversized white T-shirt and underwear. She opened each drawer and inspected the different items of clothing. She knew to spend time with her dad when he was happy because he never stayed that way.

A few days had passed, and it was beginning to be too hot for Lacy to do much of anything. She stared at herself in the bedroom mirror. Lucy grazed her face with her hand, and she grabbed the small amount of fat she had on her stomach, which she later in life realized was mostly skin and necessary for regular human function. She shifted the angle of her body to one that made her appear skinnier, practicing so that when she saw her brother's friend, she could assume that same position. She squinted and scrunched her nose; She was feeling a combination of ugly and minor appreciation for her features. She was wearing a white bikini, which had two purposes. To accentuate her new boobs and to make her tan look darker. She softened her eyes and moved her attention to her long brown hair. The curls reached below her shoulders, a new development that was only allowed because her mom was not around to chop them shorter for no particular reason. She heard footsteps coming from her brother's room. She listened curiously. She was always interested in what her brother had to say. She paused what she was doing with a hopeful expression.

"You ain't getting any prettier, let's go." Hudson laughed.

Stupid boy, she thought. She felt foolish, but she wasn't surprised by her brother's comment. After grabbing a semi-wet towel, she skipped to the living room. She caught eyes with her brother. She attempted to give off the impression that she didn't know what he was thinking. He returned a look of pretending not to know that she knew, he knew. Both of them were uneasy with the fact that she had hit puberty. Hudson, more uncomfortable than her, quickly changed the subject. He decided to pick an argument. They began aggressively discussing when the pool opened. Nothing was done in that house without emotional charge.

"We have been there before! Last year, the sign said 10am!"

"We don't know for sure, we haven't been to this one."

"That's convenient for you to say, considering you tried to drown me at that pool location, so you don't remember that either?"

"Lacy, what are you talking about…"

"Ugh!" Lacy was so worked up that she almost just did not want to go. But the thought of her brother's friend was too enticing. Dumb boys, she thought.

They made it after a 25-minute walk, and Hudson immediately threw Lacy into the pool. Pat sat on the towels, eating the PB and J's that he had packed for the three of them. Hudson was, soon after arriving there, asked to apply sunscreen to one of his lady friends. Lacy climbed out of the pool and made her way over to the chip stand. She noticed a cute boy standing in line in front of her. He was a little younger than her normal type, him being the same age as her. She felt it was okay to settle because of how blue his eyes were. She loved blue eyes. He turned around and smiled.

"Whatcha gonna get?"

"Some potato chips, probably."

He had a kind look in his eyes, and she was drawn to it. She had a wild look in her eyes, and he gravitated towards her. She felt something run down her leg. 'Oh no, oh no, oh no, fuck.' She tried to end the conversation so that he would turn around, but it was too late. His eyes found the place where blood streamed down her leg, and she began to tear up.

"Wait here."

She was thinking suicidal thoughts at this point. She went through the five stages of grief in the time it took for the boy to get a towel. Denial, anger, bargaining, depression, and then, well, actually, she never did reach the 5th stage, acceptance.

She could see her brother and his hot friend watching and laughing from across the pool. 'I hate boys.'

"Here you go."

"Thank you." She faintly mumbled trying to pretend she was invisible. The boy walked away and she began smiling. She had had a full conversation with him, what an accomplishment. The man working the snack stand probably thought Lacy was showing signs of bipolar disorder, little did he know being a teenage girl was the same thing. She walked by her brother on the way out.

He laughed so hard tears began practically leaping from his eyes.

"Awe fuck off. Pat, come on." She wasn't really upset, but she liked cussing despite it. Pat followed her out of the gate.

"Boy do I have a story to tell you…" They walked home sharing laughs and making fun of each other, the day turned out to be alright for the both of them.

Lacy woke up to the smell of Blueberry muffins wafting in from the kitchen. It was early, around 7:30 in the morning. She knew immediately that it was her grandmother, that blueberry muffins were her favorite, and that her Oma was the only one who knew that. She made them on every visit without fail. She was different from the rest of the family and seemed to understand Lucy on a closer level than the rest of her relatives. Lacy crawled out of bed with sleepy eyes and tossed on jean shorts and a loose T-shirt.

"Little Francis!" she heard her Oma yell.

They shared a warm hug and had matching smiles. The corners of Lacy's mouth reached her ears. They shared breakfast without the 'chaos of the boys' as her Oma would always say. There was a box of letters on the dining room table.

"Your father wanted me to go through these, he finally decided that the garage should in fact be an organized space. There were photos and letters and ornaments. His Grandma's face froze. There was a letter that read, 'To my love Frannie, From John Williams.'

"Who is that?" She asked with great wonder.

"Don't speak a word to your father about this, or anyone. He was my first husband and only true love."

'Holy shi..' Lacy's thoughts were cut off, she immediately was wondering what the letter said. Her Oma opened and read it silently, when she was finished she gave Lucy a serious look.

"Take this, keep safe, and keep it hidden."

"Okay, Oma, I will."

She Lacy a kiss on the cheek and explained that she had to leave but would be back soon.

"Bye, honey, I love you!" She yelled as she swiftly walked out the door.
'I love you…' She wanted her Oma's stays to be longer, but she didn't wish on foolish things like that anymore. She went out and sat in the sun on the trampoline and began to read the words that had once meant the world to her Grandmother.

~

Dearest Frannie,
*   You asked what my first thoughts were about you and at the moment I couldn't find the words. I was going through my old school journal the other day and found a letter I wrote about you before the feelings I had for you, seemed to be reciprocated by you. I thought you should know. Even though you will be married soon, I hope you keep me in your heart.*
*   She had dark brown eyes, the kind that moonlight could effortlessly reflect off of. Dark eyebrows and short golden hair. You could see she had been through*

things. It was hard to catch, you would have only known by the intensity of her face and the way you often couldn't see her ribcage move during breaths, despite the skin-tight cropped t-shirt.

I was young, naive, and a psychology major; she was a friend of a friend I was practicing on as a patient. Every Tuesday we met in my professor's office. A month went by and she didn't, wouldn't, couldn't open up. As frustrating as it was, I never could get upset with her. Her beauty was physical, yes, but that was only a fraction of it. It was the way I couldn't possibly know her. She was the epitome of a mystery. I ended up shortly falling in love with her cold heart, soft lips and the way she seemed to exist between apathy and love.

~

This letter would be burned in Lacy's mind. Everything she thought was cold and unlovable about her was so effortlessly loved about her Oma, by a mysterious man named John.

Lacy laid staring up into the sky. So much had happened and she could feel there was so much to come. She closed her eyes, at first thinking of John, her grandmother's secret lover. Then about school and her friends back home. Her thoughts drifted to the cute neighbor boy that she met at the pool. She felt for a brief moment comfortable in her own skin. A soft breeze blew over her and the trees surrounding sang her to sleep.

I Am Batman

by Dylan Frecks

I first discovered Batman when I was in Las Vegas. I went into a comic store in Las Vegas. I found the store because I wanted to get better at reading, and I always loved the pictures and comics in general. As soon as I picked up the Batman comic, I knew I had to read every single one of his comics . Batman helped me overcome who I didn't want to be and supported how I felt at the time.

I was in third grade at the time and I was someone who did bad things. For example, once I took a can of spray paint and sprayed it on some strangers' houses. I was more like a villain from the Batman comics than Batman himself. One day, I was watching YouTube videos and came across a video of Batman. It was the Batman cartoon, not one of the movies that had been made. Batman died in a warehouse in the cartoon. I found that I couldn't stop watching. The more I watched the more I learned about Batman.

As I spent more time engaging with Batman, I began to notice that my behavior was changing. I was going through a really hard time when I was in third grade. I had a hard time being around people. It didn't matter who they were. I had a hard time being around my family. This is why I think I did bad things, because I didn't know how to express my frustrations with humanity.

Watching Batman showed me how he also didn't like to interact with other people much. He lived alone in a mansion with only his butler to talk to. The only way he could do nice things for people was when he was in his Batman suit, otherwise he was alone and not social with other people. I also was not social with other people, and like Batman, I had anger inside me that I couldn't explain. People would assume that I was a waste of time, that I could never have friends or support, and that I would just start fights and issues– things that I did that helped get the anger out of me.

Just like how Batman solved all his problems, I learned how to hide myself and keep a secret identity. I started to feel more like myself, and I started to not let others make my choices for me. Although I had been through rough times, I started to get better, and I learned that I didn't need to be the bad guy. I learned from Batman that there are different ways you can express your emotions and it doesn't always have to be the same way everyone else does. I CAN be a better person. I can change people by not hurting them, just like how Batman doesn't kill– he just hurts them to make them stop or learn a lesson.

The lessons I learned were that never try to fit in or to become angry about someone who won't really change anything just start problems.

Impractical Lives

by Paulina Licea Ortiz

As a child, I watched a lot of content on YouTube that gave me a misconception of what a "day in life" is. When I was seven, I lived in a small apartment with my mom, dad, and little brother. I remember always asking my dad to use his cellphone to watch YouTube. The type of content I would watch would be DIY videos and haul videos. I remember watching Niki and Gabi and My Life as Eva on YouTube. They are women who make YouTube videos and share their lifestyles, do DIY videos, and do challenges. One day, I saw a "Day in my life" video by Niki and Gabi, and I decided to watch it. I remember observing the video and thinking those teenage girls were so cool. They would wake up, make their beds, work out, get fully ready for school, and do homework. They would do other activities like filming YouTube videos, going to the mall, and hanging out with friends. They seemed so put-together, happy, and fun. I wanted my life to be like theirs.

I recall viewing the videos and thinking my teenage years would be like that. I was inspired to be just like them. I didn't do my makeup, have a job, or have a buttload of homework like them yet. So I thought my life wasn't like theirs because I was just a child with no responsibilities. As I got older, I realized that my life was not even close to those videos. I would procrastinate, have a messy room, and sleep in. There were days when I would just go home from school, nap, and do nothing all day. I felt upset and very unproductive that my life wasn't similar to those videos of those other girls who were teenagers in 2014.

I was beating myself down for my life not being productive. I would have one amazing, busy, productive day, but then I wonder how everyone else did it every day. I would try to work hard to follow along on be productive. I would pick up extra shifts, go on runs, do a lot of homework, do chores, and cook food. By the end of the day, I had done all of this, I felt beaten down and exhausted. I essentially would not have enough time for myself or any time in general. I would continue watching the YouTube videos, which are now TikToks, and saying things like "I wish ___".

One day I was bored and I decided to record a video just like them, but I knew I was going to have a full, busy, productive day. When I realized that, I decided to record on the day I was going to be productive, which is when I knew that the other YouTube videos I had seen had been set up. It gave me a chance to think and think about how people only record the best versions of their days and aestheticize them.

The media has shown misconceptions of what people's lives "should be" when at the end of the day, we are human, not working machines. After thinking, it made me realize that it is okay that my life isn't like the YouTube videos. I mean, sure, some of them may have their daily lives look like that, but everyone has different lifestyles and goals. People only decide to show the media the good side of their lives, and it is extremely negative because it sets unrealistic standards for their viewers' lives. If I have gotten anything out of it, it has inspired me to use my planner more and time things out to have enough time for myself. It is certain to believe that it's okay to embrace your "lazy" side because nobody is perfect. All the media has shown busy lifestyles where one doesn't seem to work on themselves. Lying in bed and doing nothing is a way to work on yourself by letting yourself recharge.

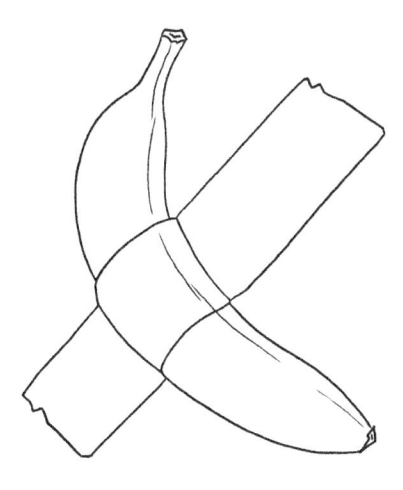

Music is Soul: A Sublime Tale

by Eva Cox

A once much simpler world has turned to the pop/modern ways of current trends and social norms. As kids grow up, they are put into their "cliques", based on music taste. Your music taste portrays your personality, style, life decisions, and friends. Even affecting your popularity. As a little girl who grew up around music as a way of art and education, little Evangeline wasn't expecting this to be a problem for her; she loved music, she confided in music, and she never expected it to ever hurt or harm her.

Evangeline loved the band sublime; she grew up with her mom playing it for her, and it clicked to her soul like no other music could. Slowly her body started morphing into this genre, and she later discovered that she couldn't find anyone with the same clique. In the high school there was the popular cliques, these consisted of pop, country, hip hop, and rap, the chill cliques that aren't as popular but liked by most, they were the reggae, indie, R&B, and dad rock genres, then there was the punk, heavy metal, emo, depressing clique that were kind of considered the weirdos. Everyone seemed to have their people, even if they were not identical genres they were always similar enough to clique together, but Evangeline did not. She tried not to let it get to her with the hope that one day she would find her people.

One evening, Evangeline was walking through the park. She did this often on her own because she didn't have many friends, but this day was different. It was gloomy out, the winds picking up at record speeds, the sun being slightly covered just enough to see an illuminated fog all around, and the weather was much more dull than usual. It was the perfect day for the depressing music kids because this was their vibe, but not for Evangeline. All was going well till she came across a tall man in a big coat. He had a dark aura around him, but lighter than the emo kids, still, Evangeline couldn't tell what genre this guy was and if he was a threat or not. She sped up her walk-in unsettlement just as she felt a tap on her shoulder, it was the man. As this man removed his hood and his gloomy jacket, Evangeline was shocked. In awe, she says, "You're one of me?!?", The man replied, "You and me are the only ones."

Evangeline, filled with joy jumping up and down, couldn't believe she had finally found someone. She was so excited for her new encounter that she didn't even realize he wasn't the same color as her. His sublime was much more orange-toned, with lots of grey and no big sun, but Evangeline didn't seem to care, she was too exhilarated. The man asks to walk with her and asks why she's walking alone, Evangeline explains that she's never found someone in the same clique as her, the man smiled with an evil grin, "Well now that we found each other, we can be best friends", he said in a creepy manner, "Why don't you come with me and I can drive you home so you don't have to be walking in this gloomy weather". That's when Evangeline started to notice, she realized the orange and the grey and the lack of a sun, he wasn't a Sublime, he was Sublime with Rome! She panicked, "Um I think I'm better off walking, my mom would get worried if I showed up in an unfamiliar car", the man replies, "You don't have a choice". The man grabs Evangeline and she starts screaming, "SOMEONE SOMEONE HELP", this grasps the attention of a little boy in a diner by the park. The little boy runs over as fast as he can, as he pushes the man and grabs the girl, he moves her behind him and punches the man in the face and screams, "Don't ever put your hands on her again!". The boy stands prepared to fight, but the man was too scared when he saw who the boy was.

The boy turned around to Evangeline, "Hi, my name is JR. Are you okay?" She stared at him with doe eyes. She was astonished, as his glistening eyes looked at her. His yellows and blues, with white skeletons and the dark purple in the middle. He was truly one of her. The boy looked just as shocked when he looked at her, and right before Evangeline was about to tell him her name, "You're one of me", JR said. "My name is Evangeline", the two looked at each other for a second then to break the silence Evangeline thanked him for saving her, "I would do it again any time", the boy says as he kisses her on the hand with a smile. A week goes by, these two are attached by the hip, doing everything together, they both were so happy to finally find another like them. As they fall in love, they spend every waking second together, cute walks through the sunny park, not a fear in the world, because they have each other. Evangeline's hope had worked. Music is what separated her from the crowds and put her in danger, but also was what saved her and healed her. Everyone has a different relationship with music, but that is still a relationship at all. Music touches everyone in different ways and can be the light and dark to anyone's days. Music is good. Music is bad. Music is love. Music is fear. Music is one's soul, no matter what shape or form it is in.

A Funny Guy, a Dark Topic, a Look, and the Boy

by Sawyer Robert Pixley

"Fifty American citizens still remain as hostages of Hamas, Biden scheduled to speak on how they…" The news reporter goes on as the boy looks down at his phone. Staring at the lights shining in sequence with the computer code, another voice projected out of the phone, more humorous and jolly. Far more interesting than the blond-haired man with brown eyebrows, speaking from a script on the tv.

"That again, really? Really?" The funnier man puts his hand up within the screen as an image comes up in the top right corner of the screen. A recurring joke on the channel, the Weezer album cover with the signature song in the background. The boy chuckles, lounging back in his chair, glancing up at his mother sitting a bit away, watching the tv. The boy looks back down.

"No no, really the gingerbread houses?" The funnier man stepping away from the camera as another meme comes in the top right corner. The boy chuckles as the bit continues. The image though, simple lights turned on in sequence by code, depicts an image of two large towers of gingerbread and a little plane molded and stuck partway in one of the gingerbread structures. The funnier man commenting, the memes rolling by, some hilarious, some falling flat, many dark, many speaking on things that could bring sadness to others. Regardless, the boy laughs as the jokes land.

Some time has passed with the boy, he has become immersed in this culture of jokes and humor. He speaks to friends just the same. Mixing in jokes as he will. Sharing funny, innocent videos to his friends as per normal. But like any passing of time, things change and develop. The humor becomes darker as he shows a friend a funny blend of satirical videos. He watches a video making fun of republican senators. He watches as funny noises play in the background of Israel's missiles. He laughs at the funny captions as a sped-up video of a cop overdosing. Horrific things in later thought and description. But hilarious at the moment.

As horrors continue in the media, the boy continues to laugh and joke. Some friends join, and they laugh and laugh together. Making fun of past presidents and joking about dictators of the past. They scorn the evils of the world from the comfort of humor. They hate the evils and bads just as much as any other. But while most talk of it in displeasure or avoid the topic altogether. In the media, in the videos, in the group, with the boy. They simply laugh about it and scorn it.

The boy was talking with friends when he recognized his difference in states. Looking and talking. Innocent too, a joke of magical unicorns no less and what each number of horned Xcorns would be like in real life in the wild. A humorous conversation of theoretical nothings. The boy's mother came by to share the information of pizza having arrived. The boy looked up.

"Thanks mum, Hey y'all let's move, we got food." The teens filed through the house to the kitchen, chatting all the while. At some point, the conversation shifted slightly to pegasuses. They spoke of them flying around New York and air traffic. The boy jutted in with his own joke, one of humor and fun, chuckling.

"Mr President, a horse has hit the World Trade Center." The boy chuckled, the friends chuckled. It was funny, at least to them. But to some, that wasn't. His mother had looked back at him from across the room. It wasn't intense or anything, and there was no big motion. She simply continued walking away with her slice. But the boy saw it, observant of her. She had not laughed, she made no sign of finding it humorous. It was small, but she seemed to dislike the joke even though it was minor.

The boy contemplated in the background of his mind, he continued to talk and joke. But he veered away from heavy topics for the moment. He talked and memed with his friends, but the thought stuck. He left it to later.

That night, surrounded by sleeping friends, he stared at the ceiling. The back of his hand resting against his forehead, his legs on top of the armrest. His brown eyes open only halfway, blinking only occasionally. He thought of why he had more tolerance for this dark humor than others, why he enjoyed jokes about some topics more than others. He pulled his phone out of his pocket with his other hand, the light of the screen as per the computer's code, lighting up his face. He scrolled through

Reddit, looking at submission groups for the memes that would appear in the funny man's videos. He chuckled and laughed. One he saw of a girl ugly crying on the side of a video of Trump's inauguration. This made him think of how he found humor while the girl found sadness. As an uninvolved party, his line of too far was far away, and he has grown used to these jokes. Whilst those more involved or less used to it, the jokes came closer to the line of offensive or saddening, or even past it. The boy turned off his phone and set it aside, reasoning that out. It's something quite obvious, anyone in the world with more than a couple of brain cells could figure that out. But it just wasn't something he had considered in the past. He thought highly of people and their ability to just 'deal with it' but he hadn't really thought about how it might affect people before such a breaking point. Or more, that people would be affected differently than he. A mistake he had made with different actions and topics before.

What was the difference between him and them? The answers came quickly, but there's only one for us to speak of. He simply interacted with a different part of the popular community. He had become different in desensitization through exposure to that humor. A funny guy on the internet wasn't the sole reason, but a whole community of jokes and humor. As people laughed away sadness at elections, murders, and dictators. They expressed their views with humor, we all do. The boy simply treaded farther into the territory of darkness.

He thought himself a philosopher speaking in intense nothings and dramatic but obvious conclusions, he added the dramatic flair of similes no longer and smiled. I then forwarded the video of the girl and the inauguration to a friend with a small chuckle at and to myself, and set down my phone.

Short Essay

How Lego Has Affected My Life

by Richard Schnur

Legos are a part of pop culture that have affected my life. I like to build Legos with my family and friends. It has helped teach me to work as a team and find solutions to problems.

Legos have been around for a long time. They are more than just blocks. There are Lego video games too. Some of the games I like are Batman Beyond Gotham, Avengers, and Pirates of the Caribbean. I enjoy them a lot because I can play them with my brother. There are also movies like Lego Batman and The Lego Movie 1 and 2. I like that the movies are funny. I think it's hilarious when Batman is grumpy.

I like to play Legos with my family. Sometimes we build Lego sets together. My brother and I built a Spiderman set. I enjoy helping my brother with Lego builds. My family and I also enjoy playing Lego video games and watching Lego movies together.

I enjoy playing Legos with my friends. We are creative and use our imagination to make cool builds. It teaches us to work as a team. Sometimes there are problems, like when we both want the same piece. We use rock-paper-scissors, look for other pieces, or share to solve the problems.

One of my favorite things about Legos is building with them. When I work on a building it helps me to read and follow instructions correctly. If I make a mistake I look at the instructions and figure it out. This helps me learn problem solving. I feel proud when I complete a build, and confident too!

In conclusion, Legos are a big part of my life. They are more than just building blocks. I enjoy playing Lego with my friends and family. We use creativity and imagination to work as a team, and find solutions to problems.

Amazing Bunnies

by Wenyu Cao

Did you know that a mother bunny can have twelve baby bunnies at once? I am going to tell you all about bunnies. Read on to learn more.

The Lifecycle

Let's talk about the lifecycle. A Bunny's life cycle starts with a newborn. After growing a little, a bunny becomes a kit. Then a young kit grows more and becomes an adult. The lifecycle begins again and keeps repeating.

Where Do Bunnies Live?

These animals live in many places like deserts, rainforests, grasslands, and snowy places. An Arctic Hare lives in snowy habitats. The desert cottontail likes hot places. The swamp bunny lives in a swampy habitat. The brush bunny lives near sticks and branches.

What are the Good Things about Bunnie?

Bunnies are smart. They have very good memories. You can teach them something and they will learn it very quickly. For example, you name the bunny and say "Come here!" and they will come after you teach this maybe 3 or 4 times. They will learn it very quickly.

Fun Facts

Bunnies mostly play and eat at night and sleep during the day. Bunnies are natural recyclers. They eat vegetables, they poop, and their poop becomes a natural fertilizer. They don't just eat carrots. They eat other things such as fresh hay and grass with leafy greens. They can't vomit. Rabbits' teeth never stop growing.

Conclusion

In conclusion, now you know a lot about rabbits. You have learned about their lifecycle, where they live, good things about them, and some fun facts. If you would like to learn more about these amazing mammals, many books and sites can guide you.

Culture and Art

by May Belle O'Connell

When I look at art it reminds me how different types of cultures can connect people. When I draw, I draw about my culture. Every culture is special and unique to their people. My culture is special to me because it reminds me of who I am. My grandma is an artist. She teaches me different art styles, she teaches me our traditional arts. In my opinion, I like our cultural art best because it is pretty and unique. I can wear beaded jewelry to the dances. I like it when people compliment the earrings I made.

It makes me feel special and unique!

II

If I didn't know my culture, who would I be? How would I know how to help my people? If my family didn't teach me my culture, how would I know my traditions? How would I know what the dances were? If I didn't know my culture how would I know I'm Indigenous? If my family didn't teach me– how would I know myself, if I didn't know my culture?

Left Out From Your World

by Cicada Pierce

Embarrassment, feeling excluded, depression, bad grades and hopelessness are all forms of sadness that can be caused by elements of pop culture. Many social lives revolve around pop culture. Kids spend hours on their devices, so kids who don't have that can be left feeling downhearted and left out. Many kids have friends taken away because of the popularity contest. Pop culture can be a positive thing, but it can also make people feel mad and excluded when they don't have a phone or something that makes them fit in. Also, sports are major, when you don't or can't play sports you get left out of many things. When you don't fit in you usually aren't liked as much and that can hurt feelings and make kids angry at each other.

You can begin to feel left out if you don't have a device and don't look at social media that much. For example, if you don't follow a youtuber or don't know any of the TikTok dances you could be left out of your own friend group. When you don't like that type of pass time, kids could start making fun of you and call you names. You could also feel left out when other kids are laughing about a certain video or short that you know nothing about. It could start feeling awkward and that you are the odd one out. Social media is fun for the kids who can watch it, but if you don't, you can start feeling really bad about yourself.

Many kids like sports and if you don't like the popular sport or just don't want to play, kids leave you out and you can start feeling like you aren't doing something right. For instance, if you don't play basketball and you hear all the other kids talking about it, you could feel like you messed up somehow by not liking that certain sport. In addition, if you are asked to do an assignment in class about sports and everyone else knows exactly what to do you could feel like you aren't smart enough and that you will fail. Sports are a big part of everyday life for many kids. When you aren't like that you can feel like you should try and change yourself which can lead to depression and feeling bad about who you are. You could start wishing that you were someone else instead of appreciating your own unique qualities.

Not fitting in can start to rule your life, thoughts and you could miss out on what you truly enjoy. Not being a part of social media can make kids leave you out. Also, not playing sports can lead to feeling disconnected to other kids. The repercussions of not liking these types of pop culture and many others can make kids angry at each other, ruin friendships and make kids feel as if they are not good enough for the world. The positive effects of pop culture might outweigh the negative if young people could find a way to include each other even if they don't have the same hobbies, but that may never be a reality.

Greta Thunberg

by Penn Kerhoulas

Problems. In our world today, we are faced with so many problems, and so many types of problems. Big problems, and little problems. But we keep trying to create solutions to our problems, and that's what Greta Thunberg is doing. One of our world's biggest problems is Climate Change, specifically Global Warming, this is when our earth begins to heat up using something called the greenhouse effect, this is when the heat that we create gets trapped in the atmosphere, it relates to a greenhouse because it comes into our atmosphere easily but then it gets trapped inside, this is just one of the many ways our earth is heating up.

At age 12 Greta Thunberg became very interested in climate change, she fought to change the way that people view climate change, not as a problem out of their control but as a problem that everybody can contribute to stopping. In August 2018 Greta started skipping school to strike against climate change, she encouraged her friends to strike with her. Her parents were both very supportive of her decisions and even now are still encouraging her. One of Greta's most famous quotes is; " Reject false hope, and demand action!" Greta has also written a book " The Climate Book." Which is fairly popular.

Every day, Greta Thunberg is striving to ensure our future. I know that Greta has inspired me a lot, she is such a great role model for young people, she believes that your age doesn't matter and that what matters more is that you care about our earth. She encourages people to try and be more ecofriendly in their decisions, and in their life habits. Greta also happens to be autistic, from the early moments of her fame Greta has always been very open about her autism, she is truly inspiring a nation of people to stand up and fight for what they want, a better, safer, more eco-friendly life. I think that Greta Thunberg is a great example of making a difference, from the age of nine I have looked up to Greta, she is truly amazing.

Female Athlete Trailblazers

by Maple Myers

Have you ever heard of Caitlin Clark, Lisa Leslie, A'ja Wilson, Breanna Stwardt, and Alyssa Thomas? Well, I have, and so have a lot of other young female basketball players. All of these women are just some of the world's best WNBA players. All of these women have changed pop culture because a lot of people and specifically young female basketball players see them on social media platforms and are motivated to do better in their sport and they look up to them as role models. They positively affect how I see myself and my mindset as a young female athlete.

In the past female athletes were hardly recognized, and when they introduced the WNBA it took a while, but they started to get more recognised and celebrated and then on August 13th, 2010, Cynthia cooper was the first WNBA player to get entered into the basketball hall of fame. Pop culture has motivated myself and many other young female basketball players in many ways. For example, I can watch the WNBA highlights and games on social media and I can look up to them as role models and want to get to their level someday. By watching these highlights and games I am provided with role models and examples of positive behaviors, as well as teaching me valuable life lessons. Also the WNBA has gotten bigger with social media so people can watch their games from home and it inspired myself and many other young female athletes across the world and it motivates us to do better. Therefore pop culture has affected myself and many other young female basketball players by giving us role models, people to look up to, and valuable life lessons.

The WNBA players have inspired me and so many other young female basketball players and changed our mindsets and changed the way we see ourselves as young female basketball players. For example, Caitlin Clark inspires myself and many young female athletes by setting many world records at such a young age and in such a short time. Also Caitlin Clarks rise to fame in the women's basketball world at the University of Iowa and in the WNBA resulted in the three most-watched women's games of all-time.

This changes our mindsets because when we see our role models setting records and doing great things it changes how we feel and play and it inspires us to get better. Overall Caitlin Clark and many other WNBA players have inspired me and so many young athletes and changed our mindsets and the way we see ourselves as young female basketball players.

Throughout this essay I have gone over the two of the many ways that pop culture with the help of social media has affected, inspired, and motivated me and many other young female basketball players. Caitlin Clark and so many WNBA players have changed the mindsets of myself and many other young female athletes across the world and inspired them to do the best they can and get as far as they can. Overall all of the WNBA players have influenced and became role models for myself young female basketball players and athletes across the world including my teammates.

How Anime Changed my Life

by Carissa Gonzalez

I first started watching anime because of my sister. I saw how my sister was into anime, so I started watching it with her. At first I thought anime was weird and cringy. I didn't understand why people love it so much. I then discovered some shows that changed the way I thought about anime. I fell deeply in love. The one I'm mad for is Naruto. I love the fighting scenes and how smooth the animation is. I admire the fact that after everything he went through, Naruto was a nice person. Even after his village outcasted and bullied him, he still cared for them very much. I love how he never gave up his dreams of being a hokage and that he followed his dream, even when no one believed in him. Naruto proved everyone wrong when he became hokage. That's why I love Naruto so much. He never gives up his dream. He followed it to the end and it shows you should never give up your dreams.

Another show I like is Charlotte. In the beginning of the anime he was rude and mean. He did not care about anyone except himself. He used everyone he found useful and got to the top of his class with his ability to possess people. Charlotte met a girl who changed him, and he became better to make the girl happy. She helped him understand his emotions and he actually started to care for people. I love that he changed himself for the better.. It shows that the right kind of people you meet can change you for the better. The other reason I am passionate for anime is because I enjoy seeing the characters change. I'm hooked on seeing how the characters evolve.

Another thing that attracted me to anime is the drawings and the animation. The eyes of the anime characters are so beautiful. I'm crazy about how some anime characters' eyes sparkle. It happens at night or when they are fighting, it's so fascinating! I'm delighted with the hair so much that you can't even understand it! I go crazy because of how adorable the hair styles are. They make the hair so cute and I fall in love. Or when the hair is down, I am delighted with how long their hair is. I wish I had hair like that! I like the cool unique effects the most! I love watching how cool they make their fighting scenes, they are so awesome!!! It makes me wanna learn how to fight too!!! I also really enjoy when they express how the characters are feeling at that exact moment.

Then I found out that anime had manga. Manga are the graphic novels of the show. At first I wasn't really interested in them because I hated reading. I watched a lot of anime and I started to notice that some shows leave you in a cliffhanger. You won't really know how many more years it will take for the next season to come out. The reason for that is because each episode costs a lot of money. It costs around a couple thousands of dollars just for one episode, and when people don't watch it they stop making the episodes. That's why I started reading manga, because it never stops until it is the end of the story. Now I'm so passionate about manga. I love flipping through the pages knowing I won't have to worry about the story stopping until it is the end of the story.. I love it so much, because with manga they put more detail in the drawings. Mangas are so much fun to read! I won't ever get bored of them! I can read manga for days on end. I'm addicted to how much adventure, romance, horror, and action there is in the stories. I cherish the drawings. It amazes me how many different manga there are. The artwork is just so beautiful. I adore manga that have color and hate when they are black and white. I am grateful to see them so colorful because they put so much detail. I can actually see the pages in full color and understand them better than before.

Anime and manga changed my life. I used to only be on social media or video games. I'm happy I found out about anime and manga; it changed my life in so many ways. I started to feel so many emotions like annoyed, surprised, upset, sadness, happiness, disgust, embarrassed, and anxious. I feel more emotions than I ever felt before. I started to become more understanding of people's feelings. Anime and manga play a big part in my life because they inspired me to start drawing more. My art style improved a lot. I started to draw manga characters and learn how to draw hair. Before, my hair drawings used to look so bad and I didn't know how to draw at all. It helped me get my own kind of style. I fell in love with drawing. I didn't care that people were better than me, I just loved the touch of drawing. I never felt stuff like this before. It felt so amazing that I started to draw every day. When I draw I feel so peaceful. That's how anime and manga have a big impact on me. I love the new me so much! Manga also helped me academically with my reading and writing skills. I was never good at reading, my reading used to be so slow. After a while of always reading, I got stronger. My reading improved so much! My spelling is getting better and also finer. I learned a lot of new words that I never knew before. This is how anime and manga changed my life for the better.

Trophy Crazy

by Bodhi Koger

Did you know that parents reward kids with trophies for just participating in a sport no matter if they win or lose? In the last few decades we've started to give out way more participation trophies. We give kids way too many trophies just for showing up to an event.

Giving kids a lot of participation trophies is bad because it doesn't give the same feeling as winning. Also, kids are rewarded way too much for participating in an event or sports activity. It makes kids think that they are just good enough and never want to improve their skills. Giving kids participation trophies kills their drive and will to get really good at something they want to do with their free time.

Many people say that giving participation trophies is good for kids' self-esteem and this trend should continue. I agree that it is good to have kids grow up with a good self-esteem but at the amount of trophies we give kids they think that these trophies have no purpose in their life. According to Dona Matthews Ph.D, "A strong sense of self is built on feeling genuinely competent in areas that matter to the individual, whether sports, painting, academics, social popularity, or something else." The feeling of getting a trophy that ties to doing nothing actually diminishes kids' self-esteem.

When Kids get trophies for just participating it makes them feel that they have accomplished more than they actually have. Once they enter the real world, the illusion that they are just as good as everyone else will disappear and the people will feel like they are lost and at sea. In the real world you can't get a job just by showing up to an interview. You have to be better than everyone else in order to establish a good career in that job. According to Passey, Jacob "Participation trophies let every child feel like they are the best, even if they aren't exceptionally skilled at that sport or competition"(Passey).

Finally, kids should not get trophies for just participating because it actually has the opposite effect than what parents think it does. It makes kids think that they are just ok and don't need to improve. Furthermore, it gives the feeling of a hollow accomplishment and actually lowers self-esteem.

Works Cited

Pavelik, Lauren. "Undeserved Praise and Participation Trophies Harm, Not Help, Kids." *LancasterOnline*, 28 Mar. 2021,

Smoll, Frank. "Trophies and Rewards Can Be Harmful to Young Athletes." *Psychology Today*, 25 May 2019,

Passey, Jacob. "Participation Trophy Debate | What Are the Pros & Cons? - Gem Awards." *Gem Awards*, 4 Mar. 2021,

Empire of Knowledge

by Zuma Kan

Everyone, everyday, all the time. TikTok, Instagram, and Snapchat. We are on social media constantly. Can we escape it? 24/7 we are evolving; our minds, our personalities, our spirits. The media is one of the most influential bodies that exists today. Does it influence us in a bad way? Good way? Both? How can we combat the bad? Encourage the good? In school, how do individuals recognize the effects, and how are we using it to help us learn? As individuals and as community members, how is social media changing the way we think, the way we act, and the way people around us act? Billions of people use social media; how is it affecting me? Us?

We are told that social media is bad. Is it? It *can* be bad, and it *can* be good. Constantly told that social media rots our brains, shoots at our mental health, and ruins social contracts. Does the reality of social media change based on the mindset of the people? When one person thinks differently than another, that creates contrasting ideas that will eventually come together as a strong solution. We continue a pattern of blaming others to make our actions reasonable. This behavior is not only encouraged by the media, but also adults. They do not stop to tell us *not* to do it. But they also do not tell us *to* do it.

"Proceed with caution." That is the mindset we are forced to have with the information being spread throughout the media. We can prove *them* wrong. We show how social media can be used for good. How to not use it for bad. How to not believe the bad. By creating an empire full of information to *help* the common folk, we are crafting a tool. Not a weapon. *We are not a weapon.*

When we manipulate our minds into weapons and we hurt other people, we turn them into weapons. That is the power of the media: everyone affects everyone. When one person uses the media for good, others follow along. When we use it as a tool, we are crafting a better world for everyone. By creating valuable and reliable information, we can change not only ourselves but the world. When we are proving the adults wrong by not getting our brains rotted or not ruining our mental health, we work harder. The biggest, most influential aspect of life today has impacted my life and the people around me. As we evolve, social media helps our evolution by adding information and strategies to our minds.

Does social media change our lives in a positive or negative way? We are working every day to start creating a tool out of the media and help others do the same. It will shape the mindset, personality, and demeanor of everyone now and everyone in the future. Social media should *not* be a weapon; neither should *we*.

Play for the Experience and Not the Outcome

by William Simms Jr

Did you know that around 28.1 million Americans play basketball from the age six and up, with the second closest sport being baseball at 15.5 million participants. Sports have a positive impact on kids all over the world. However, on the Indian reservation, where sports are all we have, it especially makes positive impacts on kids' lives. Basketball is my favorite sport; it is my happy place and it helps me take my mind off things.

Playing sports not for the outcome, but for the experience. Most people quit sports at age 13 because they can't live up to their parents' and coaches' expectations and fun is considered winning. I play sports with my friends to get a better experience and have fun. I also celebrate the small things too. All in all, for the longevity of your sports career, it is important to play for the experience, not the outcome.

There are many ways to have fun while playing sports such as celebrating the small victories, like good plays or teamwork, playing with friends: that can make the experience more enjoyable, the social aspect often outweighs the competitive nature allowing for laughter and camaraderie. Therefore there are many ways to have fun playing sports.

Basketball is my favorite sport, the reason it's my favorite sport is because it takes my mind off things in life. If I could stay in the gym shooting a basketball 24/7, I would without a doubt. I would live there if I could, but I can't so when I get in there to practice I go 100% all the time. I want to be the best at what I do so that's the reason I go all out even when I'm hurt. I've been playing basketball since I was six. I've always had a passion for it, and it taught me to pass my limits. In conclusion these are the reasons why I love the sport basketball.

All in all, kids all over the world play basketball, but on my reservation, it's all we have. If I ask kids what their favorite sport is, nine times out of ten they're gonna say basketball. When kids play basketball it takes their mind off their realities such as abusive and neglectful parents, drug and alcoholism and gives them a chance to succeed in something positive. So if you ever find yourself in a hard place, give sports a try.

The Impact

by BellaAnn King

Did you know that 95% of youth in the US from the ages 13-17 are addicted to social media? This shocking statistic shows how much kids are addicted and how much kids are influenced by social media. Not just kids from the US are addicted, kids from all around the world are addicted to their phones, internet, social media, or television. Being addicted to these things has had a huge impact on children. It shortens their attention span and worsens their mental health.

Social media has shortened children's attention span because social media platforms like TikTok or Instagram use algorithms that condition our brains to crave quick bursts of content. Also, while using the app TikTok, you are rapidly changing content and there are constant interruptions. A recent survey shows that the average TikTok video is between 12-34 seconds, with many avid users finding that any longer video is "stressful". Another thing that contributes to attention span is users are multitasking while consuming social media, which leads to further decrease attention on each task. Therefore, children all around the world's attention spans are dwindling because of social media.

Social media has made children's mental health worse because it fuels anxiety, depression, loneliness and FOMO. The more time you spend on social media can lead to cyberbullying, social anxiety, depression, and exposure to content that is not age appropriate. These things lead to children's mental health to sadly decrease, and one in seven children are diagnosed with depression. This is a sad statistic because children for the age 13-15 shouldn't be already diagnosed with depression. In conclusion, social media has made children's mental health drop because social media has caused children to have depression, experience loneliness, anxiety and many more.

Snapchat: The Social Scandal

by Skylar Groff

It's all fun and games...until it's not. Social media, the quiet killer of our generation, takes the lives of so many without our knowledge. From body dysmorphia to social standards that the world places, it's ruined our community and society as a whole. I was 13 years old when I first downloaded Snapchat to my phone. I thought that it might be a good idea and it might even help me a little. But it made me feel worse and I hated myself even more. Social media is a dangerous trap that will ruin. In this essay, I'll tell you all about my story and how social media ultimately ruined me and so many Others.

It all started on a summer day. I was lying in bed and staring at my ceiling. It was only 9am but the sun was burning on my face through the window. For some strange reason, all throughout summer break, I had been feeling depressed. I had a lack of motivation to do things and I didn't want to move from my comfortable bed. But as I was staring into my ceiling, I thought about something. I really need to start connecting with people, I feel so far away from people. So what better way to connect with people than to download social media. With some help from my mother, I downloaded Snapchat. Initially, I wanted to download TikTok but my mom said no and I agreed. After getting Snapchat, I started dabbling in what people do and what famous people indulge in hoping that I might find motivation. That's when it all unfolded.

After looking through reels of people doing things and people living amazing lives with their perfect skin and bodies, I started to feel a sense of insecurity. I didn't understand why at first because I thought it was perfectly normal to want to improve myself. But this was beyond just improving...I wanted to change everything from my appearance to my personality. Social media must be the way to go right? Wrong, it's a false cover for what's actually happening. With all of the filters on Snapchat and goofy lenses that I would play around with, they only made me feel worse because when I looked in the mirror...I saw my true self and was disappointed. When I looked in the mirror, I thought there was something wrong with myself being natural and unaltered. So much to a point where body dysmorphia was consuming me. So I talked to my mom. She told me to spend less time online and get out more. This helped so much until the NEXT issue sprung.

I was lying in bed yet again and checked out my screen time. EIGHT HOURS!!! I was SHOCKED to say the least! Then, my boyfriend at the time texted me. We were talking for a while when he said he needed to tell me something. I asked what and he told me that he did something bad. He cheated. I felt my stomach turn and I could barely speak. I looked at the text, my boyfriend still typing, and I just threw my phone down. I threw it out of my sight and away from where I could find it until I came back to my room to look for it. Walking to the bathroom crying, I felt my stomach twisting and turning with every step I took. I looked in the mirror once again and just sobbed. I thought in my heart that it was because I was ugly and I wasn't pretty like all of the model girls and that's why he cheated. So I stopped talking to him for a few days...in three days would be my time to go back to school and see him. I confronted him in the middle of the quad and laid into him about everything. He was so upset because he claimed that I "embarrassed" him in front of all of his friends.

I found myself turning into this blob of just sadness and depression. So much to the point where I started becoming a bad kid. My grades failed, I stopped talking to friends and everything was just different. All of that changed when I went online and stopped Snapchat for a long time before returning. From these incidents, what was learned is that social media doesn't make you feel happier at all...it disconnects you from others and makes you hate yourself to a point of almost no repair. So if you're in that position of devaluing yourself...just know there is a way out and that way is offline.

Social media WILL, one way or another, break you down to your lowest point. I would advise you to steer clear of social media as much as you can. Don't let a screen consume your life because my story is tragically the story of so many people globally...not just in your hometown. So don't make this tragedy yours...it will be the end of you if you do.

Political Media and How it Had an Effect on Me

by Rilynn Sauber

My father once said the worse the political climate gets the better the music gets. For me it's not just music. The media itself shows creativity and passion. Political media has had a monumental effect on my views on political ideologies and beliefs, counterculture and why I despise censorship in the media.

I was always around political media as a kid but one of the standouts was Rage Against the Machine and the movie "V for Vendetta". These exposures helped shape my opinion on the current system in the U.S. and of the world in general. I was a very opinionated kid and I loved reading about history, dystopian books. When I was around 10 or 9 my parents showed me the movie "V for Vendetta". This movie fascinated me with the intelligent masked man and the morally gray behaviors of the characters. I slowly started getting into more politically charged music like Rage Against the Machine. Whose name in the band shows the fierce politically charged ideas to change the US government. The band's strong lyrics and voice of Zack De La Rocha really got me looking at the politics of the US system. Their first album "Rage Against the Machine" enamored me with how passionate they are. The song *Settle For Nothing* is about being caught between a system and your own culture. One main point is about taking actions and not to settle for anything now or later. The song is full of emotion and anger as he talks about genocide and the American Government.

In late 70's to the 90's there were uprisings in subcultures that formed around music. They were charged full of "taboos" like punk with loud political homemade clothes and BDSM gear goth people wore to clubs. These subcultures were used as a counterculture against the normalities of these eras, The widespread beliefs of religion and conservative ideologies encouraged these subcultures to become popular as a way to rebel against a system that had been repressing these ideas. Counterculture has always been a way to resist toxic normalities in history. An example is when women dressing in pants were not allowed or when black people went into "white places" when segregation was enforced. It's important to fight for yourself and for other people's rights and go against the traditional values. Whether that be through protests or just sitting somewhere where you are not "welcomed". However these subcultures are distancing themselves from the political and radical beliefs and turning into a look that you can buy from stores. We live in a very money-based world and these subcultures have been watered down to who looks the "coolest" and even how you are supposed to look. The quote " Our town sucks; our scene rules ....To belong, you must buy into it…So we sold you metal spike bracelets….So c'mon, lets see a good fight." from Dead Kennedys speaks to me about how to fit into a box you must buy into it and how buying material objects will make you better or cooler.

Censorship has been a way to repress ideologies and beliefs that people in power don't agree with. We have seen it with the Nazis, Communist, Capitalists and Fascist. Organized groups like these have made media more simplified and digestible to the average person. Music on the radio fails to get you thinking about the real problems anymore. News outlets are spreading propaganda and have cherry picked information that gets society to believe one thing and not see the whole idea. It's not just the differing side of your opinions, it's all popular news sites. No matter what "side" you are on, you are just a dollar bill the corporations want. No one is immune to propaganda however having access to books and media that have different ideologies is needed for a society to grow. No matter if it means access to a communist manifesto or "Mein Kampf" by Hitler. Why? Access to these books and media can help add context to historical matters as well as having the knowledge to speak up against those beliefs. If you don't know what is happening or how to critique it, how can you fight against it?

Considering the beliefs about political ideologies, counterculture and my disdain for censorship came from the times of prejudice and Revolutions that showed me the path to finding my own ideas and beliefs. Political media will always be a crucial part of our society and is important to how we move forward.

Mental Disorders in Media and My Experience

by Sarah Barsanti

Suicide is the *second* leading cause of death for people from ages 15 through 20.

I was still in the midst of my childhood when my mental health first started its decline, I was 8 years old. Mental disorders like anxiety, chronic depression, bipolar disorder, PTSD, ADHD, and schizophrenia, all run within my family. Mental disorders are **very** common for us, eventually it trickled its way down to me too.

As a young child, around 2-3, I remember being punished for expressing **any** emotion that wasn't joy, if I started crying, expressing anger, etc... I'd be threatened or spanked. This emotional neglect taught me from a very young age that "emotions are bad and need to be hidden from others." I don't fully blame my parents though; my mother was working most of the time and my dad would work night shifts and would take care of me during the day. He was in the army for a period of his life and emotions were beaten out of him too, from that, as well as from his own father during his childhood.

I remember playing by myself almost every day on my elementary playground. I'd go on the swings because it was a place I could go and no other kid would judge me for being alone. I remember talking to myself a lot and telling myself, convincing myself, "I would rather be alone." and that "I didn't **need** others because they would end up not wanting to be friends with me down the road anyway." It was like this from 2nd grade up until around 7th, and in between those years of covid from 4th to 6th grade, it only made my chronic fear of abandonment from the few I did let in, and my loneliness worse. I deeply struggle with letting people get close to me till this day and put up walls within *all* of my relationships with people.

Even the people you're closest to could be in a constant battle with their mental health, and you may **never** know it.

Regularly i experience "chronic panic attacks", pulling my hair out from their roots, scratching my skin till its swollen and red, passing out, hearing loud voices screaming my name, uncontrollable shaking, and not being capable of getting enough air in for multiple minutes at a time, screaming as loud as my lungs will allow, and crying my eyes out from the pain in my chest and the stress on my body are a few symptoms i suffer from due to my chronic anxiety; in which i'm getting put on medication for soon.

I have episodes of utter rage towards everyone, and other times extreme unhidable joy, as well as periods of deep sadness for no reason. They last from days to months and if I don't have those periods I just feel **nothing** at all. I have no idea why and I *really* wish I could control them. But I can't, no matter how hard I try and I hate myself for it. I hurt my loved ones and I can't take back my words, I lose friends often. I just want to end this cycle more than anything. You might be thinking this is "just a teenage hormonal thing" because I am 15. However, the episodes I'm describing have had a long-term effect on me starting from age 8.

Online I see it all the time, people faking mental illnesses for attention or some sort of self validation on social media. It makes me infuriated to say the very least. I am forced to live my whole life with these things and they get to put it on and take it off whenever they want, receiving sympathy and pity. Not only is it incredibly disrespectful but it's also a **clear** display of a lack of basic empathy towards others. Faking mental illness or "self diagnosis" is, in my book, one of the most cringeworthy and self-humiliating things someone can do, because why, in what world is being **mentally disordered** beneficial or desirable in any way at all? It's hard to live like this every day and that's **all** there is to it. It's **not** fun at **all**.

Good mental health is extremely important and very fragile for some, after a long battle with a number of things for years I didn't want to be here anymore because I thought it would never get better for me which was only a half truth. I can change my outward views but can't change my brain. The first time I thought about committing suicide was 10 years old. The first time I attempted was in the 6th grade, I was 12. Later nobody would come to find out; this made me feel *so* alone.

Many others are struggling with similar battles, forcing ourselves to push through day by day. This is one of the reasons why people get so heated when somebody fakes mental disability or mental illness. It is so hard to live day to day like this.

There is a strong difference between **faking an illness** and suspecting you **might have an illness.** If you think you might have a mental illness, seek help, whether that's through therapy, a diagnosis, medication, hospitalization, or simply just talking to a loved one about how you've been feeling. It's hard to go through this, even harder to go through this alone.

I hope that if you are suffering in silence that you know that you are **not** alone in this. There are people who truly care and don't want you to have to feel alone in your struggle and you are not a burden for wanting to feel better. You never asked for this to be forced upon you, so you never should be forced to walk through it alone. It truly will get better, but it **only** can if **you** are willing to take that first step for yourself. You *can* do it.

The Instagram Effect

by Jaxon Davis

Since Instagram's debut on October 6, 2010, Instagram has quickly become a increasing influence on today's youth. With positive attributes like connecting with people around the world or uniting family members that live far away, Instagram has many negative effects as well. As mentioned by Nancy Jo Sales in the article "From the Instamatic to Instagram: Social Media and the Secret Lives of Teenagers" Instagram has over sexualized our young women and has caused many other crippling effects. While Instagram has a few positive attributes, the damages of Instagram far out way the good such as raising anxiety, increasing cyberbullying, escalating suicide, and depression, and causing distractions among teens.

First of all, Instagram raises anxiety among teens. In Nancy Jo Sales' article, she recounted a story of a group of girls heading to a local Dunkin Donuts after school. One of the girls could not enter the store because she had a panic attack when she realized that the kids in the store were "popular kids" that she thought would take pictures of her and use the pictures to bully her. The constant fear and pressure of people showing up and being posted on social media, like Instagram, in a negative light, is causing high anxiety and fear among teens. Some teens choose not to even leave their house and participate in society. At a local high school in Eureka, CA., Eureka High School, there are social media pages that make fun of students and blast them on Instagram and other media platforms. This has caused many students not to attend this school anymore. The anxiety of being blasted on social media and being made fun of made those students not want to go to school anymore. If this is happening at one school, how likely is it to happen at other schools? In addition, Nancy Jo Sales mentions briefly that when people post stuff on Instagram all they care about is how many likes they are getting or how many they have gotten and not what they are doing to the victim. Because at the end of the day, teens just want loyal friends that love them for being themselves and to not worry about being posted on social media in a negative way.

Secondly, Instagram has increased cyberbullying as we know it. Cyberbullying is the act of bullying that takes place over digital devices like cell phones, computers, and tablets. Cyberbullying can occur through messaging, text, and apps, or online in social media, forums, or gaming where people can view, participate in, or share content. In Nancy Jo Sales story of the group of girls, we see that the crux of the issue was the fear of being cyber bullied; therefore, the root of the issue is cyberbullying. At a time in teens' lives where they are self-conscious and full of self-doubt, nobody wants those insecurities blasted and amplified on social media through cyberbullying. Personally, I have witnessed and experienced cyber-bullying, and it is not fun when you walk into a room and people are laughing and staring at you because of what they have heard or read online about you. It tears you down emotionally and mentally, to the point where people commit suicide and do many other horrible things to themselves. Stated by Stop Bullying, an anti-bullying group that provides information from various government agencies on what bullying is, what cyberbullying is, who is at risk, and how you can prevent and respond to bullying.

Among students ages 12-18 in grades 6-12 who reported being bullied at school during the school year, 21.6% were bullied online or by text. Among those who were bullied, nearly twice as many female students reported being bullied online or by text (27.7%) as compared with male students (14.1%). An estimated 16% of high school students were electronically bullied in the 12 months prior to the survey. Nearly twice as many female students reported being electronically bullied (21%) as compared with male students 12%).

Next, Instagram is escalating suicide and depression among teens. Sales emphasizes how platforms like Instagram and Snapchat contribute to these challenges by fostering environments that promote comparison, competition, and the pursuit of validation through likes and followers. This constant exposure can lead to feelings of inadequacy and heightened stress among young users. Nancy Jo Sales notes that "social media exacerbates mental health issues, including anxiety and depression." In addition, social media creates this idea of a picture-perfect world, when life is not perfect. How many people do you know of that are like, if only I had the perfect partner? What if I had perfect parents? What if I was a great sibling or child? By Instagram and other social media platforms creating this picture-perfect idea, people begin to think they are not enough, or they are horrible because of a few mistakes they made. We are all human, and we are going to make mistakes, there is no such thing as a perfect world or a picture-perfect life. Stated by the Jed Foundation, a non-profit organization that protects emotional health and prevents suicide for teens and young adults in the United States. "42% of high school students reported feelings of sadness or hopelessness in the past year. This percentage is higher for females (57%), Hispanic students (46%), multiracial students (49%), and lesbian, gay or bisexual students (69%) (CDC, 2023)". Does this mean that Instagram and other social media platforms can or are causing depression and suicide? Stated by Child Mind, dedicated to transforming the lives of children and families struggling with mental health and learning disorders by giving them the help they need. "Evidence is mounting that there is a link between social media and depression. In several studies, teenage and young adult users who spend the most time on Instagram, Facebook and other platforms were shown to have a substantially (from 13 to 66 percent) higher rate of reported depression than those who spent the least time." A connection can be drawn between using social media like Instagram and having high rates of depression which if not dealt with, can lead to suicide.

Most importantly, Instagram causes distraction among teens. Salas' concern is that this distraction, combined with the addictive nature of the platform, often prevents teens from developing healthy self-esteem and meaningful relationships outside the digital sphere. As mentioned by Nancy Jo Sales in her article "From the Instamatic to Instagram: Social media and the Secret Lives of Teenagers", one of the girls from the donut shop story mentioned, "I spend so much time on Instagram looking at people's pictures and sometimes I'll be like, why am I spending my time on this? And yet I keep doing it (Sales 364)." This is a perfect example of how Instagram distracts teens. Another distraction Instagram causes as stated by Addiction Center; a rehabilitation center dedicated to providing caring, effective addiction treatment for those in need of help. Our services are available to everyone, regardless of age, gender identity, race, economic standing, or romantic orientation. "Instant notifications from Instagram can become a burden for young people, causing them to feel obligated to check the website and app for updates and respond to them. This can lead to even more time spent on Instagram and can end up in further increased addictive patterns of use." Another example, with the constant buzzing and notifications coming from Instagram and other social media apps, students are continually looking at their phone. Their phone must be inches away from them, or they cannot concentrate on everyday things. We see this causing legislation to come about to combat this distraction! Stated by EdSource (EdSource has been chronicling the state of education across California and wider trends across the country from pre-K to college. We believe that education decision makers—students, parents, teachers, legislators, and more—deserve access to trustworthy information driven by facts and data, not outrage cycles and misinformation)."Assembly Bill 3216, renamed the Phone-Free School Act, requires that every school district, charter school and county office of education develop a policy limiting the use of smartphones (in schools) by July 1, 2026." Extended studies have demonstrated that the use of smartphones in classrooms can detract from students' academic performances while contributing to higher rates of academic dishonesty and cyberbullying," said the authors' statement. "In consideration of California's deficiency when it comes to academic performance, as compared to other states, it is imperative for the legislature to take action to resolve this issue." This issue has become so big and bad in the California school districts that they passed a bill just to prohibit students in schools from being distracted by their phones with social media apps during the school day.

In conclusion, Instagram has a few good and healthy aspects like connecting with people that are far from each other or being friends with people around the world; however, as stated in Nancy Jo Sales article "From the Instamatic to Instagram: Social Media and the Secret Lives of Teenagers" Instagram has many negatives that out way those positives, such as raising anxiety, increasing cyberbullying, escalating suicide, and depression, and causing distractions among teens. As a society, we must do better! We must work to create a world that is free of causing harm to others and a world where people do not feel the need to hurt themselves or others. Whether limiting access to harmful platforms like Instagram or harsh consequences for behavior that tears others down, we must do better!

Works Cited

Lambert, Diana. "California passes bill to limit student cellphone use on K-12 campuses." *EdSource*, 29 August 2024, Accessed 19 February 2025.

Matta, Nadia. "Instagram Addiction: Signs And How To Overcome It." *Addiction Center*, Accessed 18 February 2025.

"Mental Health and Suicide Statistics." *The Jed Foundation*, Accessed 18 February 2025.

Miller, Caroline. "Does Social Media Use Cause Depression?" *Child Mind Institute*, 14 January 2025, Accessed 18 February 2025.

Did You Know That Having a Deaf Mom Can Be a Social Issue?

by Cameron Hayden-Davi

As you can read from the title, yes I have a deaf mom and for those who don't know, deaf means you can't talk or hear. Not a lot of people know what American sign language is which can make it really hard for others to communicate with her if she were to need help or need to ask for something. Having a deaf mom can have some challenges such as, communication barriers, different languages and differences, different cultures, learning barriers, and everyday communication.

Whenever we go out to buy something, go to the grocery store, or go to the fair it can be hard to communicate because of the communication barrier. Whenever my friends come to my house for the first time, they are really nervous and shy because they don't know how to communicate with my mom. Lastly, if we are out with friends that can hear and we are having a conversation, it can annoy my mom because she won't know what we are talking about until someone starts translating for her.

I speak two languages, English and American sign language, and with it can bring some challenges. I speak both languages all the time and I tend to forget some words in English and some words in American sign language. That can be a struggle because if I forget the word, it takes me a few minutes to remember it.

The deaf culture can be very direct, meaning they express how they feel very bluntly. The deaf culture also uses expressive communication with each other, meaning they use their body, facial expressions, and hand motions to express how they feel. Deaf people need eye contact to communicate with others because they need to be able to look at each other's body language. All of the deaf people in the deaf community have a connection with each other. There aren't many deaf people in Humboldt, and because of this, they are all super close with each other.

Since American sign language is my first language I had a really hard time learning English. As a kid I needed to get speech therapy, and I started speech therapy from

1st grade to 6th grade which was really hard for me because I thought that I was weird for not knowing English. Now I know that it was the best for me because if I was not in speech therapy, I would not have been as fluent in English. I am really happy about and thankful for my parents who made me do the speech therapy.

Every day, I speak both English and American Sign Language. Talking to my Mom is way different than talking to my Dad or friends. For example, all I have to do is say "hey" to get my friend's attention or my Dads attention, but to get my Moms attention, I have to either wave, or stomp on the floor to be able to communicate with her. When communicating to her, I have to sign at a slow to normal pace, keep eye contact at all times, and use body language when talking to her.

Having both a hearing and non hearing parent has its challenges. Over the past 15 years, I have been able to adapt and overcome each of these challenges by communicating to my Mom and Dad and doing my part to introduce the world to American sign language in my everyday life and helping others to learn different cultures.

How Pop Culture Shaped Me: Finding Light in the Dark

by Humphrey Mbugua

In the age of social media platforms like YouTube, Twitch, TikTok, Instagram, and music streaming services. They have become more than just entertainment; they've shaped who I am. I've been deeply influenced by creators like BruceDropEmOff, Flightreacts, Cashnasty, ImDontai, Penguinz0, and Solluminati as well as music artists like Playboi Carti, Summrs, Pi'erre Bourne, and destroy lonely. These creators and artists weren't just people I watched or listened to, they became a source of comfort, inspiration, and wisdom. They helped me through my lowest points, taught me to appreciate the small wins in life, and pushed me to work harder on my goals

During quarantine, I hit one of the lowest points in my life. I lost a lot of friends after we switched to online learning, and it made me feel super alone and isolated. Video games, which had been my escape, soon lost their spark, and I felt empty playing them. I was stuck in the same loop: wake up, play games, go to sleep, and repeat. I felt like nothing mattered anymore. Then I found creators like Flight Reacts, BruceDropEmOff, and ImDontai. The energy, humor, and ability to turn even the most ordinary moments into something hilarious had pulled me out of my dark slump. Flight's wild reactions, Bruce's carefree attitude, and ImDontai's perfect mix of comedy and real down-to-earth attitude and conversations made me feel like I wasn't alone. I remember nights when I had felt completely drained and alone, but then would watch one of Bruce's streams when he would be messing around on stream, and suddenly I would be smiling from ear to ear dying of laughter. It was the first time in a while that I felt something other than emptiness. More than that, they taught me to appreciate the small wins, whether that was making it through a tough day, getting a small improvement in a video game, or even just laughing at something simple but funny.

Beyond humor, some creators made me look at life differently. Solluminati was a huge inspiration for me. He was one of the biggest NBA 2 K YouTubers, but at the peak of his success, he stepped away to focus on his spiritual journey. He had stopped drinking, smoking, and partying, realizing that those things weren't what made him truly happy. Seeing someone at the peak of their popularity wit everything money, fame, and success, admit that he still felt alone even with all of the success and things he had accomplished. Made me reflect on my own life at the time I had drifted away from my own faith unsure of what or who I believed in. But watching Solluminati take control of his life and focus on what really mattered, which was his mental and physical health. This had made me want to reconnect with my own spirituality. It reminded me that happiness isn't about what you have, it's about what's inside. BruceDropEmOff also taught me an important lesson about believing in yourself even when nobody else does. When Bruce started on his YouTube journey, he was failing school, arguing with his parents, and had people doubting him left and right. But he kept going, he bet on himself stayed true to who he was, and now he is one of the biggest streamers getting multimillion dollar deals. His story really resonated with me because I'm not the smartest student, and sometimes it feels like dreams are out of reach. But I knew through Bruce's story and through his determination and will to push through all the doubt and make it then why can't I?

Watching Bruce succeed motivated me to work harder in school and stay consistent in the gym. Instead of looking at my struggles as a sign to quit I started seeing them as part of the journey. And as all journey's it's the build up and everyday goals you set for yourself that end being the funnest parts, and Bruce showed me to fall in love with the process even on the hard days. Instead of looking at my struggles as a sign to quit, I started seeing them as part of the journey. I used to get discouraged when I didn't see instant results, but Bruce's story reminded me that success isn't about overnight wins; it's about stacking small victories until they turn into something bigger.

Music also played a huge role in shaping who I am. Artists like Playboi Carti, Pi'erre Bourne, Destroy Lonely, and Summrs influenced not just my music taste but also how I carry myself. Carti's music and interviews shaped my confidence and style, making me feel like I could express myself however I wanted. Pi'erre Bourne's at the time and still is retro arcade game beats had changed the music scene, especially with the combination of his beats and Carti's vocals. Which at the time was unheard of in the music industry and shunned by the older rappers. But with their rebellion against the old style and old wave, I decided to do the same with how I dress. During quarantine, when I felt lost, I would turn on Summrs music. His songs about pain, loss, and struggle made me feel understood. I remember one night when I was down on myself and really questioning everything I put on Summrs music, and for the first time in a long time, I felt relief listening to his lyrics and the beat that just carried his words like a gust of warm wind gently kissing your cheek. I cried fully, I felt all of my emotions that had been stored in me for a long time. His music didn't fix everything, but it made me feel like I wasn't alone. It reminded me that pain is temporary, and even the worst moments will pass.

People often say that social media is toxic and that pop culture is shallow. But for me, it was life-changing. It gave me joy when I had nothing, it showed me a new perspective on life, and it helped me build confidence in who I am. It pushed me to work harder in the gym, stay consistent in school, and focus on my goals. Creators and artists aren't just entertainers, they are storytellers, motivators, and sometimes lifelines. My experience matters because I know I'm not the only one. There are so many people out there just like me who have been saved by a song, a video, a stream. In a world that can feel overwhelming sometimes all it takes is a creator who makes you laugh when you're at your lowest or an artist whose music speaks to your soul. Pop culture isn't just entertainment, its connection, inspiration, and proof that even in the darkest times there's still light.

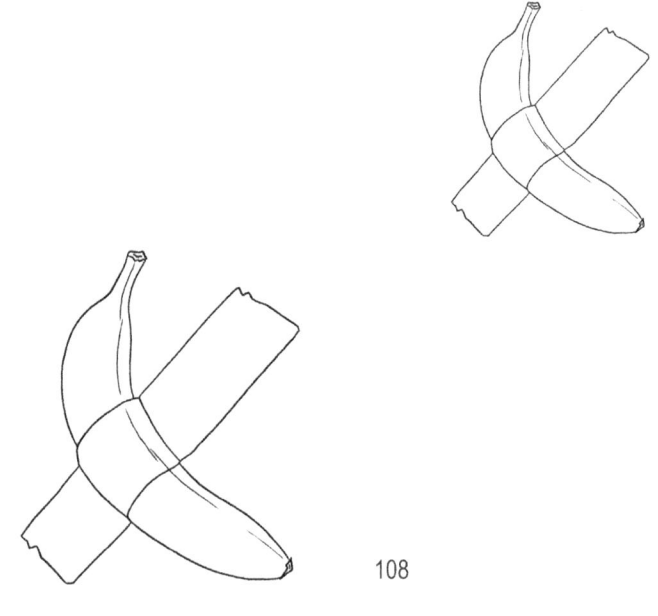

Black is Beautiful

by Fallyn Miller

Historically Black Colleges and Universities have had a tremendous influence on pop culture. From television, film, traditions, and music showcasing the HBCU culture, and the experiences of Black students. This has all led to increased enrollment and recognition at HBCUs and the black community. When you connect HBCUs and pop culture they have been influenced by each other for decades and will continue forever.

When I look at myself I see a black woman, a black woman that's going to do amazing things. When I'm sitting in a class and I notice I'm one of the only or the only person of color it hurts a little bit. When I think back on my 12 years of public education I've never had a colored teacher. And I don't think that's anything someone should go through

The traditions of HBCUs have influenced pop culture by their marching bands, traditions, Greek life appearing in movies, music, and all over social media. It even happened at one of the biggest events in the U.S., the Super Bowl. Not only did the famous Human Jukebox band from *Southern University's* open the whole super bowl. Kendrick Lamar had a super powerful rendition making it a significant moment for black culture.

I'm attending a HBCU in the fall. When I toured I felt at home. The smell, the weather, the food, the people all made me feel so at home. The culture and traditions were all over campus and there would be no place I'd rather spend my next 4 years. When "The Cosby Show" came out in 1984 and "A Different World" in 1993, the rise of American higher education increased by 16.8 percent. During this same time period HBCUs grew by 16.8 percent meaning it was 44 percent better than all higher education.

Music is a huge part of pop culture as well as HBCUs and black culture. Many celebrities have been touched by the "HBCU experience". For example Drake referred to HBCUs in these songs going back decades ago like when The Notorious

B.I.G talked about Howard University in the 1990s. In 2018 the most elaborate HBCU celebration was put on by Beyonce at Coachella, she had the marching band, a step team, she truly inspired the audience and put a spotlight on the true excellence of HBCUs.

The excellence of HBCU is something only some will ever feel in their lifetime. I am one of the few that will get to experience it. Celebrating black excellence is what it is and it's something I'll be proud of and carry the pride of forever. *Southern University at New Orleans* has a long beacon of academic excellence making it an ideal choice for my higher education journey. One of the many reasons I'm drawn to SUNO is its commitment to healing everyone and making a true difference in the world both big and small. The university seems to care for "the whole person" and this resonates deeply with my values. I believe that any education extends far beyond the classroom. SUNO's diverse range of programs and supportive family-like environment will provide me with all the tools I need to develop not only as a nurse but also as a person. It will make me an engaged member of society.

When black culture and HBCUs connect the outcome is amazing. HBCUs in pop culture will and have forever had a legacy of stealing the spotlight. Black culture and HBCUs have changed how everyone views black education and culture.

Rock n roll came from black culture, jazz came from black culture, hip-hop came from black culture, soul came from black culture, it all came from black culture so next time you listen remember where it came from. Black culture is not a fashion trend, black is love, black is rich, black is power, black is life, black is me.

      Black. Is. Beautiful.

Works Cited

HBCUs in Pop Culture: 6 Iconic References Through the Decades. *HBCU Lifestyle – Black College Living*, April 03, 2024

H.B.C.U.s Have a Spirt All Their Own. Pop Culture is Paying Attention. *The New York Times*, May 21, 2022

Women in Pop Culture

by Evelynn Snow

Women around the world struggle. Their struggle has become normalized. Women and young girls alike everywhere struggle to break from the helpless ropes that bind them. The ropes of expectations and fear. Most women are treated like they are lesser than others, they're treated with a grain of salt. The usage of social media has hurt the image of young girls and women. It has instilled a fear that doesn't need to be there, lodged expectations in the throats of young girls and women. It has hurt the way women see themselves. It has hurt the way I see myself.

The use of derogatory words towards women has become vicious and dehumanizing. A term that has surfaced the internet is "Femoid" aka "Foid". It's a term that was made to basically categorize women as "female-like". The use of "Oid" is dehumanizing and is used in words like Humanoid which means something is human-like and has the characteristics of a human, but they're not quite human. I've yet to hear a term used towards men in that way. A term calling men less than a man but something like that. It hurts to see women called something that is female-like. People who use these terms see women as less than what they are, a woman. A while ago I found a women's TikToks of her reading comments that men have left saying disgusting things about what they want to do to "Foids", how "Foids" don't deserve rights or a choice to bear a child, how "Foids" are weak and the men is strong. It really hurt. It hurts to see that this is how men out there view women and they voice this out on social media. How there could be girls and women out there who take their words to heart. I remember googling this term and thinking how ridiculous it is that we have reached a point where we are seen as even less than a woman, we are seen as woman-like. It must make it easier for men to harass women if they don't even see them as a woman.

Girls who play online video games aren't even safe from the predatorial eyes of others. Girls who usually play video games hide their voice just because of the things that are said to them, things that are normalized among some men online. Many girls who speak up online are called out for it and there are either one of two reactions. One, the woman is sexualized for being a "gamer girl" and asked disturbing questions about her body or explicit questions that I'm sure nobody wants to hear or two, the woman will be harassed and told to get off the game.

I've spoken up in game chats before and I've had both reactions a couple of times. I've mainly had men talk to me in a sexist way, I haven't been told the worst of the worst but it's enough for me to stray from the game chat. I've heard the phrase I'm sure most are aware of, "Get back to the kitchen" or "make me a sandwich". I've had both said to me and although it's a childish thing to say and I don't take it to heart, it's just an unnecessary thing for people to begin saying. Although again, the phrase is childish it can sprout other ideas in young boys' minds. Video games are very popular among boys and girls everywhere. In those instances that someone is telling a girl to get off the game and "get back to the kitchen" that boy who's playing that game and hearing this be said might think it's okay to say all that. Peer pressure is very real and can even happen with kids. My little cousin always tries to act like me or say something she thinks will appease me. I understand that little kids want to be like the older kids and act like them. Who's to say these young boys won't pick up on saying comments to girls online because they heard someone else say it?

Some other prominent issues I've seen sprout from TikTok and Instagram are the young girls who grow up too fast. There are young girls out there, some in elementary school, who are buying skin care, makeup, talking about getting their acrylics done and being strict on their appearance. This has bled into the minds of young girls everywhere telling them that they have to be model perfect. These children watch these teenage girls or even young adults and see how they have a skincare routine and they wear lots of makeup, these young girls feel like they need to do that too. Most kids now have a phone and access to social media, their young minds can't comprehend what they see. The trends they try to follow for being the perfect woman are unrealistic. Girls are shown online that they need to be pretty in order to be loved. They need to be pretty in order to matter. They need to be pretty and smart in order for anyone to take them seriously. I remember seeing these trends on Instagram and TikTok, these young girls showing their morning routine and what they bought from Sephora. When I was a little girl I had Monster High dolls, and a scooter I would ride around my sidewalk. I had no care In the world. I would wear sketchers with a long skirt and a My Little Pony shirt. It's rare to find those same little girls now. Social media has slowly poisoned the next generations by telling these young girls you better start now or you'll never be pretty. This is such an unfortunate set of events to watch go down. Watching *kids* worry about if their contour is smearing, watching these *kids* dress in crop tops and leggings. Playing pretend and dressing up is one thing, but when they are posting and believing what they are seeing then it's a different story. The story of pop culture.

Pop culture can be all sorts of things, slang, songs, fashion trends, movies, actors/actresses. Pop culture can also be a blind eye. Pop culture can be the mistreatment of women and girls. Some without realizing it while others are made with malicious intent. Women being seen as lesser has been an issue for generations. Pop culture has only amplified another struggle for women to get through. The struggle to prove themselves. The struggle to show they matter. The struggle of a watchful eye. The struggle of Pop culture.

The Impact VSCO Girls Had on Society

by Shyla Mosier

During 2019 there was a big trend on VSCO girls. VSCO girls were viewed as basic girls who wear scrunchies, carry around water bottles and say "and I oop" but in my opinion it was more than that. VSCO girls brought awareness to the dangers of single use plastic and how it harms our planet and the animals that live in it. During the short-lived trend, VSCO girls promoted environmentally friendly products and brands that donate to non-profit organizations and are eco-friendly.

One product that was widely promoted in the VSCO era was metal straws instead of single use plastic straws to "save the turtles" people may not know that many marine animals are killed each year because of single use plastic, not just turtles, and even though the trend did not last long enough to make a huge difference it educated a lot of younger people and made them aware on the environmental dangers we face because of plastic. A specific memory that i have of metal straws is that during the trend of VSCO girls my entire family decided to get metal straws. We got many metal straws so that they would be available to us wherever we were. My mom had a collapsible straw in her car for when we go anywhere. To this day I still have at least five metal straws at my house and it did cut back on our plastic use as a family.

Another thing that was popular within this pop culture trend was reusable water bottles, such as Hydroflasks. There have been many water bottle trends throughout the years but VSCO girls were the only ones who made it about environmental awareness. In one single day there are 1.3 billion single use plastic water bottles that are used in the world. So reusing a water bottle every day for a year is not only environmentally friendly, it also saves money. I remember having a Hydroflask with a bunch of stickers on it and eventually Hydroflasks were out and Stanley cups were the next big thing. Water Bottle trends go super fast. Stanley cups came out of nowhere and then they were everywhere and everyone has one. While they may not be trying to make a difference on purpose like VSCO girls were trying to do, the water bottle trends are still cutting down on single use plastic daily.

The VSCO trend did not last as long as some people expected, and that may be due to the hatred that everybody had for VSCO girls. The mockery of how they dressed and acted became more popular than the trend itself. People made videos of them impersonating VSCO girls and would make fun of someone for not using a plastic straw to "Save the turtles Sksksks" If people would have been more accepting on the matter, instead of putting everyone who participated in this trend into harmful stereotypes, then we could have made a real difference in the amount of plastic that ends up in our oceans. The trend would have ended up being more effective and people would be more willing to listen to the damage we are doing to our planet if people didn't make the trend a joke. I personally heard people make jokes about killing turtles just because they thought the trend was dumb. I never considered myself a VSCO girl but I don't think they deserved the amount of hate they got for advocating for the animals that cannot help or stand up for themselves. We as people need to realize that we need to take care of the planet we live on and the animals that reside among us.

VSCO girls were an important part of pop culture because it brought awareness to environmental problems that not everybody knows about. Turtles are an endangered species like many other marine animals because of the single use plastic that is ending up in the ocean which animals get stuck in or mistake for food. VSCO girls showed that there are people in our generation who care about the environment and there needs to be more references to environmental awareness in pop culture. This is important because trends within the new generations will be the most beneficial in the long run and can make a difference in the world if enough people are aware and educated about the topic. There are over 900 species of marine animals that are affected by plastic entanglement or ingestion and awareness needs to be raised to make a difference and save not just the turtles, but all animals.

Pop Culture: A Short Essay

by Patti Henderson

Pop culture has significantly influenced my life in many various ways, shaping my interests, personality, and style. From my music taste to fashion and social media. Pop culture has made its way into my everyday life, often guiding my preferences.

Pop culture mainly was introduced to me in my childhood, around early elementary school. I grew up in Thailand so the differences between American culture and Thai culture were very different, despite the differences the videos I would watch on YouTube in Thailand did not change when I came to America in second grade. My dad is American and would show certain American values and traditions. I still remember staying up late with my dad and him showing me the most popular YouTube songs. I remember hearing Nicki Minaj, Shakira, and Katy Perry. I would dance while he would play the songs and that influenced me into wanting to sing. I would sing songs on my mom's phone and record myself. Later when we first moved to America I auditioned with my dad and sang in front of the whole school while my dad played the ukulele.

I've transferred many times since our move to America, I transferred twice during elementary school and twice in middle school. Middle school was a rough time for me, growing up in humboldt county also made it worse. I was introduced to many things that I've never seen before. Eventually going to a public middle school in Humboldt county, I fell into the wrong crowd, I started hanging out with kids that got bad grades and were disrespectful. Since I was young it was hard for me to make friends, I've never had a best friend before and I always wanted to be one of the popular girls starting at a very young age. So when I started hanging out with the wrong crowd I didn't mind as long as I had friends. I would try to fit in and look like them and some of my friends were African American, they had beautiful hairstyles and I would spend hours scrolling on Pinterests and TikTok finding one I wanted to try, eventually I found a hairstyle that was two Dutch braids with purple hair added. I tried out the hairstyle and my friend did my hair, unfortunately my hair type is not in any way similar to African American hair so my hair fell out when I woke up the next day. I then tried out for the cheer team in seventh grade to try and become more popular, but instead of fitting in, I was the odd one out of all the cheer girls that have been cheering their whole lives. Eventually I got bullied so badly and got tiktoks made of me so my dad transferred me to a private catholic high school where one of my childhood friends went.

Seventh and eighth grade were when Covid-19 started and I spent a lot of time on social media. I tried all the new trends, I remember making makeup tutorials, trying new recipes, and trying new clothes. Eventually high school started and I just wanted to fit in and going to a new school was weird again. My freshman year I stopped being friends with my childhood best friend and tried fitting in with the popular girls, after forcing myself so hard to fit in by buying every single trendy outfit I saw on tiktok, straightening my hair every day. Following every makeup tutorial on YouTube I finally became one of them. I was so happy, I finally got what I wanted until something wasn't enough. I saw how all my friends were getting so much attention and I wasn't. I wanted to know what was wrong with me, I noticed they were all blonde so I got highlights and started dressing like them. I then got some male attention, enough for me to get a boyfriend. I dated him for a year and it was so toxic and abusive, it was so much for me to handle at such a young age. Eventually it got so toxic to a point where I had no friends and was only " allowed" to hangout with him and only him. It got to the point where I couldn't handle it anymore and broke up with him. I got stalked, threatened, etc. The relationship went into my Sophomore year so at the beginning of junior year I had to start from scratch.

I tried fitting in with that same group of popular girls and they were not as accepting. At this time in high school, they started going to parties, drinking, and smoking so I could only hangout with them if I brought vapes, alcohol, or weed. I was kind of a joke to them, one of the girls really didn't like me and spread a rumor that I slept with one of the girl's boyfriends. That rumour turned the whole school into hating me so I had to get out of there. I then transferred to Eureka High and I had nobody, I was so scared and I transferred so late in the year. I became best friends with a girl in my pottery class and would hangout every day until Senior year started. We were like sisters, we did everything together. We listened to the same music and we even dressed the same. My senior year I gained a sense of self, I dyed my hair back to brown, I did my makeup however I wanted to. I lost that to a boy and that boy taught me how to be myself, which I see as a blessing in disguise. I would try different things to impress him and overtime he caught on and taught me that no matter what I looked like he would still love me. I stopped trying so hard in the mornings to curl my hair and instead I learned how to take care of my natural hair and watch TikTok on the right products. I still wear my curly hair every so often since it's so time consuming to take care of. Instead of wearing whatever I thought he liked I just wear sweatpants and a hoodie and he doesn't love me any less. When I would hangout with guys before him, I would try to put on a fake persona that made me look boring. My boyfriend saw right through it and I just was myself and learned that was perfectly fine.

Overall pop culture has had a big impact on my life positively and negatively, yet I still reach more towards pop culture for my sense of style, I still definitely have gained a sense of self and I wouldn't recommend introducing pop culture at too young of an age because I don't want a middle school girl to be scrolling on Instagram seeing models and expecting herself to look like them. When I eventually become a mother I will make sure my kids are comfortable to be themselves and to love themselves.

Anti-Social Media

by Cole Zeller

Pop culture is something that always has been and always will be a thing that lives and evolves with human beings. Today our pop culture has become something that all previous generations would not recognize because we now have social media as its driving factor. Specifically, social media is often used for people to post about everything in their lives. Even the small things that no one cares about (like what you ate for dinner) will be posted and this is what is in our pop culture has become today. *Not* interacting with social media has impacted me by making me happier as a person and bringing me a sense of relief because I don't have to spend lots of time stressing over the issues that come with it. On top of that, this choice has given me the opportunity to be closer to family and friends that I enjoy spending time with and taught me a new way of looking at the world.

Another clear impact of my choice to not use social media is an increase in my happiness when compared to others that frequently use it. Some good examples of this are people that post something and spend the rest of their day looking at how many likes they got, and if they don't get the amount of likes they want, then it ruins their day. This is such a silly way to go about your days; people that are constantly posting on social media are stuck in a trap that wants them to keep engaging in their platform as a way to feel good about themselves through a dopamine rush. But at the same time the only thing that it actually does is bring stress into their life. So by not involving myself in this cycle I have had the positive effect of being able to focus on what is important and right in front of me. Another example of this is my mom, who loves to do activities with our family and always loves to take pictures of us having a great time. This in itself is a great thing to do, and in fact I love getting to look at these pictures years later and see how fantastic of a time we have, but what I don't think is a good thing is the amount of posting that she does of that content. I know that sounds weird to say and as a middle-aged lady she does not have the same negatives that come with teens staring at their likes, but what her problem is something completely unrelated. The problem that I find with that is very simple, while the posting of social media is supposed to bring us closer to those that we know and what to have seen, it has actually done the opposite. Social media may be an efficient way to get an update out to a large group of people but it's not very personal and therefore doesn't create close connections.

When we post on social media the idea is that the people that we know are seeing what we are up to and thus bringing you closer together by knowing what everyone else is up to. I would argue that this is doing the opposite; the days of talking on the phone or going to get a meal with someone you know or love is gone. People now see everything that the people they know are up to and do not feel the need to make a phone call to an old friend they haven't talked to in a year because they are still "close" after looking at each other's lives through posts. This phenomenon has played out in front of me many times with people that are my family or friends, when their so-called social media "friends" haven't actually talked to them in years. I choose to not use social media and thus I can't see what others are posting and also don't post anything. So I am still in the practice of calling the people that I care about once a month that aren't in my everyday life to check up and see what is happening in their life and tell them about mine. This act of calling or doing an activity with the mindset that you are there to see what each other are up to is a much more personal and refreshing way to keep up to date with people.

The final impact of social media and its role in pop culture is the "keeping up with the Joneses" effect. Meaning that beyond close friends and neighbors, everyone is competing to try and give the perception that they live a perfect life with no flaws. I have seen so many clear examples on trips that I have gone on with extended family or had friends tell me about where they talk about the family fighting the whole time and people crying. The thing is when you see the post about this trip there is nothing about that, it is all about how great of a time they had. It's all sunshine and rainbows, making people think that's how life should be. Another thing is that people post about the expensive things that they buy, and then people think that they need to buy nice things too, even though they don't actually need the items, just to "keep up with the Joneses." Both of these experiences with social media have influenced me to no longer believe what people show me on social media and also to not care about the posts. If you spend your life trying to live other's lives or a life that gets likes from other people you will be stuck in a life that will not bring you any happiness and instead will only be a blip in someone's scrolling that might give you a like.

The absence of social media has had an unbelievable, positive effect on me as a person, and with that I have learned what truly makes me happy. The rejection of both social media and the use of it to stay within the loop of pop culture has made me a happier person that is even more connected to people. But not the people that could care less about me, the people that I am up to date with in their lives are the ones that truly care about me and that I truly care about them. It has also taught me to take almost everything in life with a grain of salt. Every person in the world has a reason behind what they are saying or posting, in order to know what is actually happening you must find that out before coming to any conclusions about the truth.

Overall I believe that social media as a tool for people is too good at doing its job. Social media companies want you to spend as much time as you can on their app and thus make them money, so they pull you into spending time on them. They show you the things that you want to see and thus make us as a whole very divided. Today people are trapped in echo chambers where they cannot accept any other opinion because they only see the ones they agree with due to the algorithms. If people were to take a step back and look around they would see how blind everything that they see on social media makes them. So in conclusion the most impactful thing that social media as a facet of pop culture has on me is that I have learned that you must take a step back in life and see what is truly happening. You must live in the time you are given to its fullest extent and not worry about what some random person is commenting on your post. In life you may lose or you may win, but you'll never be here again; so you might as well enjoy what you have now, personally connect with those you care about, and take a moment to love yourself for where you are in life.

Social Motivation

by Alex Jimenez

Various aspects of pop culture impact the lives of many in both positive and negative ways. Controlled by the people who influence it, popular culture shapes our society. Pop culture, specifically social media, has positively impacted my life. It has made me a stronger and better person mentally and has forced me to challenge normality. Social media has also forced me to become more critical and pay more attention to what I consume, and it has influenced me for the better by changing my mindset.

Social media for me has been mostly inspiring. Creators such as David Goggins and Rich Piana, who have shared their stories and shown how they have come out of dark places throughout their life, and whose stories serve as inspiration to people from all walks of life. Have used social media to influence my life positively, and I have started many new habits as a result of hearing these stories. Such as getting up earlier to go to the gym, reading, going for runs, and many others, which have been exposed to me through social media, and influencers who have spoken to me. Social media, a broad term, has impacted me for the better and has forced me to be better and challenge myself. It has introduced me to being all I can be.

Secondly, although many consider politics being present in social media to be negative I see it as a positive. Politically social media can often be misunderstood due to people trusting what they see on social media before considering reviewing the content they see. Due to social media's ability to work with the consumer, the content that you see is in theory related to what you agree or disagree with, therefore more and more people are stepping away from traditional political opinions, and allowing who they are as a person to influence them, rather than someone else. I feel that social media has changed my personal political opinion, I also feel that as I have gotten older, I have reinforced the ideas that I believed in. Personally, social media has shown me the difference between liberal and conservative ideals, and the radical left to the radical right, in today's day and age where politicians are more radical than ever, and more comfortable expressing their radical ideals more than ever. Social media has shown me both sides of the ball. And has allowed me to create my own opinions on how I feel about controversial topics regarding the world.

On popular social media apps, such as TikTok, Instagram, or YouTube, the content which is recommended to you, is influenced by your previous watch history. Therefore by that standard the content that many consider toxic, or manipulative, or the content that people see as unrealistic or over-the-top, is presented to you by your choice. How Social media influences you is your own choice, I have also experienced content that I thought was unrealistic, however instead of viewing it as unrealistic, I decided to take it as a challenge, people may say that getting up early is difficult and that nobody does that, because what the point. I have also thought that way before, however, once I changed my mindset and stopped the negative thoughts, I took it as motivation. I realized that it is possible to get up early and work harder than the people around you. All of this I learned from social media, but it starts with yourself, social media itself is a tool and should be used to better your life, but to use it as a tool, you have to be willing to change your mindset, as this will change the media which you view.

Social media, for me, has been nothing but positive. My experience, much like the experiences described by the positive influences that I mentioned before, is another example of people being moved, and influenced by people who have triumphed from adversity, rather than accepted it for what it is. People must become stronger and more resilient, and I feel social media and pop culture is the first place to start, by changing the way you look at these tools, and start to use them to better yourself.

The Influence of Sports Betting

by Dallin Baker

I chose sports as my topic to talk about gambling and sports betting. Sports betting/gambling is one of the most done activities in young adults. A study survey done by NCAA.org shows that 58% of individuals aged from 18-22 have been involved in at least one sports betting activity. Sports betting is a big part of pop culture because a big majority of people who are over 18 like to bet on their favorite sports teams. Pop culture made an impact on sports betting on people because it's more engaging to bet on sports because people like to attempt to win money while also watching their favorite team. Lots of sports betting companies pull in young people to bet by using sentences such as " Join now for a free 50$", which can be very convincing to people who don't know the dangers of gambling.

Sports betting has become popular through pop culture. For example, sports betting wasn't as common before the advancement of technology. Before phones were a thing, the ways to promote sports gambling weren't the best. When phones and social media became more popular, sports betting became very popular because of pop up ads. One another thing that influences sports betting is all of the celebrities that are sponsored by these betting companies. Some memories I have of sports betting was watching the super bowl for the first time in 2015, I saw ads for sports betting. Sports betting has become so popular because of people's loyalty to their team or their willingness to win money. Gambling is a serious problem and needs to be talked about more.

Another way that sports betting has become popular is from fantasy sports. Things such as fantasy football brings people who weren't as involved in football before, then making them more involved. Like I mentioned before, the advancement of technology allows for more coverage of the sports betting apps. Through apps like TikTok, Instagram, X(twitter), Snapchat, and Facebook, pop up ads are common because they allow for a person who doesn't know about sports, to get more involved through sports betting.

Another example of sports betting coming up is from recent years. When I watch any NFL games, they show advertisements such as, "Join now and refer 5 friends to get free credit", this shows that they want to advance their app to other users so that they can get a lot more money than they're actually giving you back in free credit. The last example I have is during the super bowl, there was an ad for a user to win some big money prize like 5 million dollars if they spend over 100$ on the sports betting app on that day. That convinces users to gamble a good amount of money for a tiny percentage chance of actually winning the big prize.

So, in conclusion sports betting is related to pop culture because of gambling. Gambling relates to pop culture through people promoting the sports betting apps. Celebrities such as Mike Tyson, Christiano Ronaldo, Neymar, Etc. With these popular celebrities everyone knows them so most likely if someone promotes something and you know the person, you will believe that the thing they are promoting is credible.

My experience matters because I've seen some of my family members lose a good amount of money because of gambling on sports betting. Gambling has many effects, when people win a lot of money they then put most of the money they win back into gambling. When people lose most of their money they are left with barely any money and will either gamble the rest of their savings away or be left with nothing. So in conclusion, pop culture affects people because they get advertised with gambling and get addicted.

Made in the USA
Columbia, SC
02 June 2025